THE HAND OF THE WICKED

To
Don,
thank you for your
support and your
freindship —
all the best!
Bob Gray
11/17/17

THE HAND OF THE WICKED

Bob Young

Published by Eagle Veterans Services LLC, Augusta, GA
www.EVSLLC.net
www.bobyoungbooks.com

ISBN-13: 9781505889642
ISBN-10: 1505889642

"Deliver me, Oh my God, out of the hand of the wicked, out of the hand of the unrighteous and cruel man."

Psalms 71:4

Dedicated to
John L. Nau III

PREFACE

——◆——

A FEW YEARS AGO, I wrote a book called *The Treasure Train,* a historical novel that wound its story around events connected to the robbery of a great treasure known as "the missing Confederate Gold." The collection of real-life people and events I came across in my research defied believability. You've no doubt heard it said, "Some things you just can't make up."

The Treasure Train left loose ends that cried out for more detailed examination, and three years ago I began researching for a companion book. While collecting source material, I met an elderly, crippled freedwoman named Nellie West. Her brutal murder came at the hands of two white men in rural Taliaferro County, Georgia, in the summer of 1865.

As a criminal matter, the murder case was clearly decided. Who killed Nellie West and why they did it were not in question. After reading the transcript of the military commission that heard the case, I had no doubt the killers were appropriately sentenced to be hanged. I thought that would be the end of the story. However, what I had found turned out to be only the beginning of something much bigger. My research was like peeling the layers off an onion.

Fleshing out Nellie's story took me across the electronic impulses of the Internet; into the halls of the Library of Congress, the National Archives, the Georgia State Archives and various university collections; and onto back roads of rural east Georgia.

My research revealed a political system operating in the chaos of Reconstruction that placed little value on human life, especially if the victim happened to be a freed slave. I found the gallows could be an especially fearful ending of someone's life, but it was never a given that a prisoner, especially a white one, would swing for his transgressions, no matter how egregious. And I found that the government we rely on every day to keep us safe was an unworthy protector of basic human rights.

The Hand of the Wicked is the true story of the murder of Nellie West. The principals are all real people. Much of the dialogue is replicated as it was originally presented in court testimony and personal writings. Two main characters—Timothy Wood and Josiah Stephens—were created by me to help advance the story and give it context.

Nellie West's voice has been silent too long. She comes alive again in the pages of this book. Perhaps the telling of the full measure of her story will give her the justice her government denied her in 1865.

Bob Young

PROLOGUE

———◆———

WITH THE BOMBARDMENT OF FORT Sumter in South Carolina on April 12, 1861, the South embarked on an irreversible course of separation from the union of states. One by one, Southern states joined a chain of secession that would lead to the creation of the Confederate States of America and a bloody four-year conflict.

Anything associated with the North could no longer be tolerated in the South, not even the most American of all holidays. As the war dragged on, Independence Day provided a glimpse into the soul of the South.

Augusta, Georgia
July 4, 1861
Let us commemorate the day by no noisy demonstrations—by none of the pageantry of the past; but rather by silent tokens of respect for the memories which it brings, and the great principles which it recalls....

Then, when the dark clouds, which now hang heavy over our young Confederacy, shall have passed away, and the bright sun of peace and prosperity shall once more shine over us—as we fondly hope it will soon—we may once more celebrate this glorious day with loud huzzas—with the roar of artillery, and the clangor of martial music—with military pageants, and oratorical displays—and not only this independence day, but with the new independence day of the Confederate States of America.

Daily Constitutionalist

———◆———

Augusta, Georgia
July 5, 1862
The Fourth passed off this city with very little demonstration of the noisy sort. Our citizens were too painfully exercised with the thoughts of absent friends in our army at Richmond to be particularly jubilant. The bulletin boards about the printing offices, where the latest news was promptly posted, were surrounded with eager readers all day.

Augusta Chronicle & Sentinel

———◆———

Augusta, Georgia
July 4, 1863
Once more in the cycle of years, we are called upon to note the recurrence of the anniversary of the independence of these States. The occasion brings with it mingled pleasure and repugnance....Should we not hold the occasion doubly sacred, in that we have again achieved our independence of the rule of the oppressor, and though still unrecognized and still excluded from the community of nations, are today a de facto power, able to hurl our victorious hosts upon the country of our foe, and to strike dismay into the hearts of those who would fain become our conquerors and rulers?

Augusta Chronicle & Sentinel

———◆———

Well into the third year of the conflict, Southerners had become disillusioned by brutal fighting, rising casualties and depravations at home. They bore the brunt of the fight because it was playing out on their farms, in their villages, in their homes. They were weary, perhaps, but not defeated. The Northern holiday was now more than ever a Southern rallying cry.

Augusta, Georgia
July 4, 1864
The same motive—the right of self-government—that produced the Revolutionary War inaugurated the revolution of 1861, and the result will inevitably crown our arms. Harmonious action, unity of purpose, and zealous perseverance in the cause of freedom will accomplish the independence of the Southern States just as certain as night follows day.

The wisdom of our rulers, the sagacity and skill of our Generals, the bravery of our soldiers, and the patriotism of our people will soon be rewarded with peace and independence.

The 4th of July 1865 will, we firmly believe, dawn upon the Confederate States as one of the acknowledged powers of the earth, for we see through the smoke of battle the eagle perched on our victorious standards.

Daily Constitutionalist

———•———

All things must end, even a war. And this one did in April 1865. After those years of hard fighting and sacrifice on the battlefield, the editorial writer's boast of just a year earlier rings hollow. Southerners are now subjugated under the North's oppressive hand of Reconstruction.

Independence Day struggles for recognition in the former Confederacy. The freedmen—that new class of American citizen—and the occupying Northern armies embrace this day as one of celebration everywhere in the South from small villages to large cities. But alas, July Fourth largely remains a Northern holiday.

Washington, Georgia
July 4, 1865
The Yankees gained it no favor, waking people up before day with their vexatious salutes. Every good rebel, as he turned over in bed, gave them and their day a silent execration for disturbing his slumbers. I never heard such hideous noises as they made—but I suppose it was only proper that the reign of pandemonium should be celebrated with diabolical sounds.

Our negroes all went to the mongrel barbeque....

Diary entry of Eliza Frances Andrews

Fort Warren, Massachusetts
July 4, 1865
The war, which every true friend of liberty has deeply regretted, has been terminated, it is true....Where is the boasted liberty that makes the people of the United States the freest on earth? Why am I here without warrant, or charge of a crime? Why are the forts, prisons and bastilles all over the land, this day filled with thousands imprisoned as I am? How is it that no man is safe in the utterance of his sentiments unless they be in accordance with the views of those who rule in almost absolute sway from the Canadian to the Mexican borders?

Diary entry of Alexander H. Stephens

Augusta, Georgia
July 4, 1865
Southern whites, hard-pressed to find redemption on most any day, view this day as a celebration of Northern conquest. Perhaps, that is

why only two national flags are seen flying among the shops and store-fronts here on Broad Street, the major thoroughfare through this city that is Georgia's industrial hub. One of the flags, put up by the *Augusta Chronicle and Sentinel*, is so large its stars and stripes stretch across the street between two buildings. "The largest ever seen in Georgia," the newspaper proudly brags.

The first sign that something is special about today is the sun-rise firing of weapons in regulation salutes by the military garrison in Augusta and by the soldiers camped on Shultz Hill in Hamburg, just across the Savannah River. Such noisy volleys of cannon and musket have not been heard since the guns fell silent at Appomattox and Bentonville months ago. Their loud booms long reverberated through the length of the river valley. The thick grey smoke lingered a bit, as if a morning fog.

By default, this year's Independence Day is primarily a negro holiday, a day to mark liberation from the bondage of whites in a manner similar to whites using the day to celebrate their liberation from the peonage of a European monarch. The freedmen find support in the armed Union troops attending to martial law and in local Unionists, their neighbors who had abandoned the idea of secession from the beginning.

Promptly at nine o'clock this morning a parade of celebration be-gins. Under the direction of R. Cummins, the Marshal of the Day, the massive procession rolls out from the grove below the Scale House on Broad Street. The thunderous beat of the Drum Corps of the 331st U.S. Colored Troops, all dressed in their bright blue and gold braided uniforms, reverberates off the buildings along the way, more felt than heard. Following is a collection of formations of occupying Union soldiers from New York and Connecticut, assemblies of cler-gymen, many in their clerical robes, societies and trade groups, and school children.

Trailing the procession with their own displays of pride are 4,000 freedmen, in every shade of skin color and manner of dress. Another 3,000 freedmen are lining the streets to cheer on the assemblage.

The procession snakes its way along a dusty Broad Street, and as the line passes beneath the newspaper's flag, military officers proudly salute. Loud rejoinders follow. The marchers proclaim their sentiments on banners held high into the morning breeze. One reads, "Lincoln, the Father of Liberty and the savior of the country." Another proclaims, "Disunion and Slavery no more." Yet another, "Freedom and Equality."

The procession turns off Broad Street at Kollock Street, then over to Greene Street, and concludes its march on the parade grounds, a massive field of green grass and tall, shady oak trees next to the cemetery. The parade grounds had been a focal point for military exercises and patriotic rallies during the war. But today, music, prayers and readings of the Declaration of Independence and Emancipation Proclamation are announced to the thousands of freedmen who fill the field to proclaim the arrival of the 89th anniversary of the founding of the United States.

Rev. James Lynch, a prominent minister in the African Methodist Episcopal Church, sets the tone for the occasion from a speaker's stand festooned with evergreens and patriotic banners, including a national flag once carried into battle by colored troops. Wearing a black robe decorated with a cross and a dove, the pastor takes on a conciliatory tone. He charges the freedmen to "cultivate and cherish a spirit of friendship and respect for the whites." And he has more to convey.

"Our late struggle was fought by heroes both North and South," he intones. "And we acknowledge Alexander H. Stephens and the others who breasted the storms of action until they were swept from their moorings by the mighty currents of popular delusion."

"But the white man is not alone in building a new foundation for the Union. No, he is not," Reverend Lynch submits, rocking his head side to side, his voice rising in a crescendo. Speaking directly to the largely absent white population, he argues, "The colored man, if he is not unduly hampered by prejudices and restrictions, might do something for humanity, too."

He draws cheers from the men and women, young and old, who listen closely and hang on his every word.

Mopping the sweat from his balding head with a royal blue handkerchief, Lynch continues with a message to his negro audience: "All the colored man is asking for is justice. But neither this right nor any other can be secured by idleness, vagrancy or lawlessness. And you cannot accomplish anything by violent measures but must rely on moral considerations alone and patiently bide the hour of your complete deliverance."

With a glowing tribute to the late President Lincoln and to the red, white and blue of the Union flag, Lynch takes his seat amid a storm of applause.

His message is as much religious as it is patriotic. For years Reverend Lynch has been telling the faithful that the hour of their deliverance from the ravages of sin is near. Today he brings them the good news that their day of deliverance from the bondage of slavery is at hand.

Other speakers extol the significance of the day, and representatives of the Freedmen's Bureau offer instruction on the new order of law and society in the South.

For a time, the parade ground is the center of life in this city, as it bakes under a bright but scorching summer sun. Not even the pesky no-see-ums can deter the emotional responses of thousands of new citizens on what is the first public celebration of their independence, appropriately capped off with a magnificent fireworks display

However, for all the hope, optimism and promises made by a seemingly endless line of official speakers today, a dark cloud continues to build in the hearts of many who feel wronged by the outcome of the war and remain resentful of the new status of the negro. Their bitterness will only continue to grow as new pronouncements are made and laws enacted to elevate the former slaves at the expense of their former masters.

In the countryside around Augusta, both negroes and whites are unhappy and disillusioned. Within days of the celebrations that elevated negroes and offended whites, people who hoped for a better life will see their dreams shattered.

Some wounds cut deep and are slow to heal; others become infected and fester. Oppressed people find no safety from the hand of the wicked.

———◆———

CHAPTER 1

West Plantation
Raytown, Georgia
July 13, 1865

"NELLIE WEST, YOU GET BACK into this house right now." John Brown's angry voice boomed through the rooms and hallway of the house and out into the yard. The sound was so loud, in fact, that his neighbor, Seaborn Acree, could hear that voice a half mile away at his place! Even Acree would know from the outbursts that Brown was not a happy man. "Must be trouble with the coloreds, again," Acree thought.

"Nellie, I know you hear me," Brown shouted as he came through the kitchen, where he startled the women who were preparing breakfast, and then approached the open back door. "I want you back here right now to get your chores done," Brown bellowed, as he charged through the doorway and out of the house. He was clearing a direct path to the negro woman who was headed out to the field to join her family, totally disregarding her overseer's commands.

So, as the morning sun broke in a fan of red and yellow rays across the horizon and the joyous celebration of Independence Day drifted off as a memory, Nellie West headed out of the main house to the corn field, oblivious to her overseer in noisy pursuit.

What set these events in motion? Brown's wife, Sara, had some washing for Nellie to do. But Nellie claimed she couldn't wash. She said she was laboring under both a toothache and a headache.

"Where are you going, woman?" Brown demanded, following her across the dusty road next to the house and into the field.

"I'm going field-hoeing," she hollered back, breaking her silence.

"Why didn't you come to my wife when she sent for you?" he asked.

"My feets is sore, and I's not disposed to work for your family ta'day." Nellie never slowed her pace, hobbling along on a shoeless and bandaged right foot that had earlier suffered a deep cut.

"You God-damned old bitch," Brown said, his voice getting louder. The gap between the two was narrowing. "If you do not go back to the house, I will pick up a chunk and beat your head to jelly."

Brown was even closer. "You black bitch. I told you to get back into the house, and I mean now!!" Then he shouted, "If you don't listen to me, I'm going to pick up something and knock your old damn brains out!"

By this time, Nellie was with her sons in the corn field. But she would find no safe harbor among family. When Brown began to close in on her, she pivoted and headed back toward the house. Brown's steely green eyes locked on Nellie's son Rafe. Brown's scowl was met with a look of worry on the lad's rounded brown face.

Brown was not a man big of stature, but what he lacked in size, he made up for with a commanding voice and mean determination. His bright plaid shirt and tan felt hat set him apart from the other hands in the field in their bleached cotton work clothes. And Brown's well-worn black boots and faded blue dungarees sent a message of a man who spent a lot of time in his fields. Too much time there, the negroes would argue.

As Brown trailed Nellie, he was waving a gnarly, three-foot-long brown pine branch, a stick that in the hands of Brown could do a lot of damage to someone. He cursed and scolded his prey. "Damned old bitch," he shouted as they approached the house. "Damned sorry nigger." Brown's vocabulary was rather limited when he was speaking to the negroes.

She had been to see her children in the field, but was that enough? "Who do you want to go to?" Brown demanded, as they met in the yard near the well between the main house and the cook house.

Nellie stood there in silence, her brown eyes staring toward the ground beneath them, never making eye contact with her tormentor. "Mister West," Nellie finally responded. She hesitated a moment. "Yes," she affirmed, "I wants to go down to Mister West. Can't stay with you."

The surly Brown was taken aback. He worried how the plantation owner, Rev. Tom West, might perceive an unhappy negro worker at his door. "Wouldn't you rather go to town to the Yankees?" he offered as an alternative, perhaps not initially processing the potential consequences.

Nellie thought for a moment, scrunching the weathered jet black skin on her face. "Yes," she replied firmly, her eyes opening wide. "The Yankees it is!" A half-smiling expression crept across her face. She thought to herself that the soldiers could do more for her and her family than her former owner was capable of. After all, West put Brown where he is. "Yes," she thought, "I'll go see the Yankees."

The federal troops had arrived to establish martial law in nearby Washington about two months earlier. Capt. Alfred Cooley's company of colored soldiers from the 156th New York Volunteer Infantry was currently garrisoned in the town and had spent much of their time there keeping the peace and taking loyalty oaths. And they had plenty of work to do. Washington was a key stop along the trail for soldiers returning home from North Carolina. The town was a crossroad, literally and culturally, teeming with Confederates headed home to a new life and freedmen seeking their new future.

Brown had to think fast. It wouldn't be helpful to him to have a bunch of Yankee soldiers snooping around the farm. And there's no telling what Nellie might say to them.

A note. Yes, a note! Written permission was needed for slaves to leave the farm, but for a freedwoman? In Brown's world, yes. He would have it no other way.

"Bitch, I'll give you a note to take to the Yankees," he said in a low, menacing tone.

Suddenly Brown lunged at her. He grabbed the pink-flowered hand-kerchief Nellie had around her neck and drew her short, slight frame close to his. Then he seized her around the neck and began choking her violently with both of his hands.

Brown's family members and the other negroes who had gathered 'round were shocked at what they were seeing.

"You just don't know who you are fooling with." Brown's hands easily closed tighter around the woman's slight neck. As they did, he wrenched her head side to side.

"I've had about as much of your insolence as a body can take," Brown fumed. He tightened his grip even more.

Christopher Reese, a neighbor lad, was visiting the overseer's house that morning, and from near a doorway, he saw the confrontation play-ing out in the yard before him.

Reese watched Brown continue to choke the woman, shoving her and shaking her, his grip never loosening.

Then Reese announced, half laughing, half seriously, "If I had my way about it, I would take a chair and knock her damn brains out!"

At once Brown released his grip and dropped his hands down to his side. Nellie fell to her knees. She was gasping for air and taking deep breaths. She rubbed her neck with her hands. It's a wonder she survived, but then, again, it's a wonder any of the negroes survived an encounter with John Brown.

"Go get your things ready to get out of here," Brown thundered.

He turned to Reese and instructed, "Write her a note to take to the Yankees. Get that nigger out of my sight." Brown then stormed across the yard and back into the house.

Nellie slowly got back on her feet and dusted the red clay powder off her dress. Trying to regain her composure, she walked away toward her own house down in the quarters. She had gotten only a few steps when she turned and called back to the main house for her 9-year-old daughter, Lucinda, to come with her. Lucinda was inside preparing for her daily chore—swatting the flies away from the table while the Brown family ate their breakfast. Lucinda heeded her mother's call and started to leave the house.

The exchange only made Brown's anger run deeper. He called out to Lucinda to come back to the house and ordered her into the kitchen. No, if Brown had his way, Nellie would not see her family before she left the farm.

In the small log cabin that she called home, Nellie changed her outfit, putting on something more fitting for travel—a long, sackcloth-looking gown in brown hickory stripe, tied at the waist with a raw cotton string in nine knots to ease her stomach cramps. She combed the kinks out of her hair with a card and wrapped her handkerchief with the pink flowers around her head, tying it into a tight bow in front. Then she collected some bread and a few other items into a cloth to carry on her trip. Before leaving, she sprinkled some sulfur, salt and pepper into her left shoe to ward off any evil spirits that might be lurking along the way. Finally, she closed the door and locked it, intending to leave the key with her family on the way off the farm.

Nellie went directly back to Brown's house to get the note from Reese. But Brown was still there and wasn't through dishing out instructions to her. Nellie said she wanted to leave through the field to say goodbye to her children and give them the key to her house.

"No, you will not go by the field," Brown demanded. Sometimes it seemed that Brown dished out orders just for the sake of tempting his negroes to cross him. "You will use the straight road and go out through the gate."

Then he added, "You go into *my* field, I'll give you a portion and kill you!"

Nellie might have been mouthy, but she was still somewhat obedient. She left the house—note in hand—and as she walked out of sight down the road, Brown turned to Reese saying, "I'll give five dollars this morning to see the damned old bitch hung." Reese did not appear alarmed by what he had just heard. He silently nodded in agreement.

With Nellie out of the way and breakfast now behind him, Brown proposed to Reese that the two go hunting. They grabbed their guns and headed down the road toward the creek, the same road Nellie had taken a short time earlier to begin her journey to see the Yankees.

By now the sun was well above the horizon, warming the landscape, and the morning air was heavy with humidity. Brown and Reese were already working up a sweat. Reese's faded and torn blue coveralls were blotched with patches of sweat. He was wearing his grey cavalry hat to keep the sun off, which seemed a futile effort. Brown occasionally pulled a red bandana from his pocket to wipe his face. There was simply no escaping the intensity of the building heat.

They'd walked about 200 yards when Brown broke the silence. "It will never do to let that damned old bitch go."

Reese replied, "I don't know why you had me write that note and let her go. You don't need the Yankees involved in your business."

Brown turned to Reese, who was a good foot taller than his companion. "I cannot afford to have her go to the federal authorities in Washington and give them any kind of report."

Reese nodded in agreement and started to speak. He was interrupted when one of Nellie's daughters came into view driving the cows.

"Quick, into this cane patch," Brown instructed, pointing to the tall green shoots on the right side of the road. "She won't see us here." They ducked into undergrowth and walked through the cane down to the railroad bridge at Harden's Creek without being seen by young Julia.

"You know, C.C., you're as much into this as me." A puzzled look came across Reese's tanned face. He couldn't imagine how he was involved in anything with Brown, let alone a dustup with one of the negroes.

"I should not have let that bitch leave," Brown grumbled. He gripped his gun even tighter, recalling his choking Nellie earlier that morning.

Reese haltingly asked, "What do you mean I'm into this as deep as you?"

"You threatened to slap her this morning." Brown's statement resonated with his young friend. Yes, he had threatened to slap her, but people don't get into trouble for such talk. Or do they? That would give him something to think about as they continued their trek.

Encountering a fence, they climbed over and stepped out into the road.

"We need to see whether she set out for Washington or not," Brown announced. "Let's follow the road for a bit." He kept along the side of the road, walking in the grass. Reese, on the other hand, took off down the middle of the road, kicking up puffs of dust. That rattled Brown to no end. "No! Not in the middle, you idiot. Walk along the side of the road in the grass." No sense in leaving tracks to show they had been there.

When they came up to the wooden slat fence for the cow pasture, Brown climbed over and whispered for Reese to jump over and stay with him. But before he could climb the fence, Reese looked toward the railroad tracks and saw Nellie. There she was, all right, with the handkerchief on her head and a small sack in her hand, hobbling along the tracks on her bare right foot.

Brown instructed Christopher to go quickly across the field toward an old house. But Reese hadn't gone a hundred yards when Brown called to him again, this time to go across to the railroad tracks to see if Nellie was headed in the direction of Washington, about nine miles distant.

Reese ran to the tracks, stopped beside them and stood, shoulders down and hands on his knees to catch his breath. Looking up, he found Nellie coming toward him, indeed going in the direction of Washington. When Nellie saw him, she mumbled something Reese couldn't make out. She then turned around to head back toward the Raytown depot about four miles in the opposite direction.

Brown caught up with her at the intersection where the railroad tracks met the road. "What are you up to woman?" Brown asked. Nellie said she was going to the Raytown station to get on the train headed to Washington.

"Where's your money?" Brown asked. "You need money to ride the train."

"Don't have no money but I's goin' anyway," Nellie replied, her head bowed and eyes staring at the ground.

"Damn you," Brown shouted. "I'll carry you!"

Nellie abruptly turned away and resumed her walk along the railroad tracks, again turning back in the direction of Washington. Brown and Reese were now following her, carefully walking the rails, cradling the rifles they had brought along to hunt squirrels.

Brown started muttering, seemingly to no one in particular. "It will never do to let her off and report to the Yankees. These damn niggers can swear any man's life away."

Brown paused a few moments, then remarked, "A good place to kill her is at the bridge over Harden's Creek."

Brown turned to Reese and said, "If you shoot, I'll shoot." This was the first time Brown's prey for the morning hunt became clear, by directly engaging Reese to kill Nellie. What would entice the baby-faced boy with the flowing blond hair to join in this scheme? A thought crossed Brown's mind. "I'll give you my daughter, if you will."

That got Reese's attention. He was sweet on Caroline, Brown's stepdaughter, and indeed just that morning had come to the farm to pay her a visit. The fact that he could get Brown's support in his romantic pursuit was quite tempting. But the lad did not say anything in response; he just pondered the offer.

They continued to follow Nellie along the track. Brown insisted for a third time: "It will never do to let her go off."

Abruptly, he offered a challenge to his young companion. "Shoot, damn it!"

The window of opportunity was open. It was now or never if they were going to put an end to Nellie's mission. Reese did not respond, no doubt still fearful from Brown's admonition that he was in trouble for just threatening the woman.

"Woman," Brown called out to Nellie. "I'm going to carry you over to Captain George Flint's place."

"I knows what you's g'wine ta do, Massa Brown," Nellie hollered back, raising an arm and shaking a finger in the air. She kept walking, looking straight ahead, never giving her pursuers so much as a glance.

"Yous gwine ta fool me," she said, as she seemed now to taunt them.

An old pig path opened up off the side of the tracks, and Nellie veered from the tracks and onto it. She followed the path into the trees and undergrowth ahead, all the time picking up her pace as best she could with her injury limiting how fast and nimbly she could move.

Time was quickly running out. It was becoming more apparent to Brown that she might just get to the Yankees after all.

"Shoot," Brown bellowed to Reese. "Shoot! Shoot!"

Brown was standing about three or four steps behind Reese when the sound of the explosion from the young man's musket reverberated through the trees, sending birds to flight and startling even Brown. Reese slowly lowered the gun from his shoulder, and the smoke began to clear. Nellie was still upright, but stumbling more so than running. Had the ball hit her? She leaned forward and struggled to keep moving away from her tormentors in a desperate effort to escape certain death.

With Nellie still on her feet, Brown was getting desperate. He stepped closer to Reese and tried to hand the boy his own gun. "Use this one," he offered. Reese refused to take it. He had remembered Brown's words, "If you shoot, *I'll* shoot," but events quickly were not playing out that way.

Nellie meandered about 30 yards farther down the pig path and into what was commonly known as the pine field, where she finally collapsed. She lay silent, except for the raspy sound of her lungs gasping for air. Her body was sprawled on the undergrowth, her arms and legs motionless. Bright red blood was splattered on the back of her dress.

Brown and Reese cautiously walked up to her. Brown called out to her: "Nellie." There was no response other than the gurgling sound of each of her attempts to fill her lungs with life-giving air. "Nellie. Nellie," Brown again called out. He pushed at the body with his boot.

Looking over at his mentor, Reese responded, "She's dead."

"Come on. Let's get out of here," Brown urged, as they turned to flee back out the pig path. "But, wait!" he called out, both of them stopping short.

The sound of the woman's breathing became a bit stronger, more audible. Brown exclaimed, "The damned old bitch is not dead!!" Reese still didn't pick up on the sign of life, but Brown did. He told Reese to hit her with a rock. "Damn her, she's putting on deceit." Faking her death, Brown thought.

Reese picked up a small rock. He was reluctant to throw it, insisting, "She's dead!"

"Throw it!" Brown demanded. Reese finally yielded and pitched the rock toward the body, hitting Nellie on a shoulder.

"She's not half dead," Brown insisted, now leaning over the body for a closer look. He stood back up and removed his hat to wipe the sweat from his brow. "She'll get up after we go away." He urged Reese on. "Hit her again!!"

"No, I'm not," Reese responded in a most determined manner. Was he now having second thoughts about what he had just done—shooting that defenseless old woman? "You do it yourself if you want anyone to do it," he sternly told Brown.

Brown struggled to keep his acolyte engaged. "You have done shot her. You may just as well finish her."

Brown had a persuasive way about himself, and Reese was not immune to succumbing to his demands. From Brown's point of view, Christopher was the killer, not him. The boy finally put his stubbornness aside to reach down and pick up another rock.

The size of the rock did not please Brown.

"Here, give me your gun." Brown snatched the squirrel rifle from Reese's hand. "I'll hold it for you." Brown then pointed to a bigger rock, pushing Reese toward the stone. "Damn it, throw down that small rock and take this larger one." Brown picked up the rock and handed it to Reese. This time Reese threw the rock firmly. It struck Nellie in the head with a loud cracking sound as it gashed her skull. The bloodied rock tumbled to a stop on the ground next to her head.

Nellie moved no more. Nellie breathed no more. Her lifetime in obedient, yet tortuous, servitude to others had come to a violent end. No matter that she was on the very cusp of enjoying new freedoms she so desperately sought.

Brown finally seemed satisfied. He laid their guns down on the ground, then approached the now lifeless body. He pushed it with a kick. No response. Yes, the deed was done. Brown reached down and, grabbing onto the dress and skirt, dragged the body about 15 steps, head first. He then stuffed the body under a limb on a pine bush. And so it was that the trees would stand sentinel over the remains of Nellie.

The pine field was known not only for its tall, towering trees filled with bright green needles that stood like masts on a tall ship, but also for the saplings and seedlings that sprang from the brown cones that littered the ground. The pine field was lush and green in grass and undergrowth. It was not good ground for crops, but excellent for grazing cows.

"You done a good thing today, boy." Brown was effusive with his praise for Reese, patting him on the back as they walked out of the field through the pig path.

Reese enjoyed a reputation in Raytown as the town troublemaker, but never had he endured anything so dark and permanent as killing another person. Naturally, he had shot at Yankees— the enemy—during that time in the Confederate cavalry. He was a soldier and was trained to kill other soldiers. But Nellie's murder? No, this was pure wicked meanness.

Reese tugged on Brown's arm, moving in closer to him. "Never tell on me, now that you have gotten me into this," he pleaded to Brown.

Brown locked eyes with the lad, who dropped his grip, and assured him, "I will shed the last drop of my blood in my body before I will do it." Reese seemed satisfied with the response.

The two men went off through an old field in the direction of Raytown, where Brown proposed they hang around all day at the depot. Reese did not like that plan; he wanted to go home and put this day behind him. About a half mile along the rail line, they climbed a fence. The choice had been made—they were now on the road headed to Brown's house.

They detoured down to Hanline's Creek, where they wet their heads and washed their faces. Brown took a misstep crossing the creek and ended up in water up to his knees. He didn't appreciate his misfortune one bit, and Reese dared not laugh, even though the misstep provided a brief moment that morning that could have taken the sting off his feelings of guilt. It wasn't long before they had to stop so Brown could shake the sand from his boots.

When they approached the house, Brown saw a group of colored boys. In a loud voice he started cursing them.

He confided to Reese, "I want them up at the house to hear me coming. Make them think we'd been out in the field all day looking for hogs."

"Mister Brown," Reese said, "There haven't been any hogs in that field since the oats were cut."

"You mean until today, of course," Brown replied with a wink.

Closer to the house, Brown saw a young woman washing. He would use her to continue to build his cover story, telling her that when the negro boys came in for lunch, she should have one of them fetch a mule and chase the hogs out of the oat patch.

By the time they arrived at the house, Brown and Reese found that quite a few folks had gathered. It was time for the midday meal, and the house was filling with family and friends. Reese's father, William, was there, as was Brown's stepson, Jimmy Garrett. The women brought in quite a feast from the cook house. Unfortunately, given the lack of success in the morning hunt, there was no squirrel—or hog—to serve.

After socializing over lunch, the men all departed for another round of squirrel hunting, leaving the women and the help to clean up. The men were gone until late in the evening. At the end of that long day with Brown, Reese was ready to go home. But Jimmy Garrett convinced him to stay the night with the Browns. Actually, he didn't need to do all that much coaxing with Caroline in the house.

In a quiet moment after dark, John Brown walked Christopher from the house out to the feed lot.

The two stood silently, looking up at the black sky dotted with bright stars. The moon, fuller than most nights, was high above them and casting a glow that brightened the landscape. A concert of raucous cicadas entertained them.

Brown began in a low, soft voice, his eyes fixed on the night sky. "You know, we should get an axe and go and cut the body up."

Reese looked over to him and stepped back. "What!?" he exclaimed. He was in disbelief of what he had just heard. The boy had spent the better part of the afternoon and evening trying to put the images of Nellie's dead body out of his mind. He didn't need Brown revisiting the matter. "I do not wish to go over there."

"It ought to be done," Brown continued, oblivious to Reese's rejection of the idea.

Reese did not respond further, and they retired for the night. The next morning, Christopher left for home.

Brown tended to business on the farm Friday and Saturday. He had given the negroes holidays on those days for getting their crops in. Nellie's family used that time to look for her, but they found no sign of her, and nothing had been heard from her. With all the rumors that the whites had spread among the freedmen about how Yankees would abuse negroes, there was much apprehension about what might have happened to Nellie, had she made it to Washington.

By Sunday, three days since the murder, Brown was feeling a bit more confident. No body had been found, and Reese was apparently keeping his mouth shut. Brown was ready to get away from the farm and spend a bit of time with what friends he had, neighbors Silburn Acree and W.D. Pittman among them. They and the other menfolk met up at Sandy Cross, a community hangout named for the two sandy roadbeds that intersect there.

Stories about hunting and tall tales about the big fish that got away were always topics. A game of cards always would be welcome. Not a lot of money would change hands in these games, what with the weak harvest coming in this year. Most of all they liked to talk about the war that was and how it might have ended differently if they had been in charge. The men didn't like the new system of free labor. For sure they didn't like visits to their farms by Union soldiers.

It wasn't Brown's nature to let a good story go to waste. He felt he was among friends, so the tale of an overseer tormenting a crippled old negro woman might prove to be the high point of the afternoon. The presence of a couple of bottles of corn liquor would dull any thoughts to the contrary.

All these men were farmers, and they had their own stories about trying to get negroes to work under the government's free labor system. As Acree later recalled, Brown shared with everyone within earshot his problems with Nellie. "He said he took hold of Nellie, and drew her up to him, and shook her, and he jerked her handkerchief off her head.…"

Whether anyone was impressed by Brown's boasting was not apparent, remembered Acree. "I judged, from the way he talked when he told this, that he was very angry with her at the time he shook her."

Pittman got an earful from the braggart too. "Brown was talking so loud and boasting so much that I could not help but hear it! Brown said he caught hold of her and choked her, that he gave her the note and that she started off toward Washington."

But even friends like Pittman were shocked when Brown went so far as to give a demonstration of how he manhandled the woman. "Brown caught hold of Mister Booker somewhere about the breast and shook him to show how he shook Nellie," he said, while holding his own clenched fists about chest high and shaking them vigorously to demonstrate.

Booker was taken aback by the demonstration, his wire-framed glasses tumbling from his face to the floor. It was all he could do to keep from spitting the juice from the plug of tobacco he had wedged between his cheek and gum right into Brown's face.

Milton Saggers was shocked when he saw Brown grab their friend. "I think he was talking about the negro woman Nellie, and I noticed Brown seize hold of Mister Booker somewhere about the chest. Brown was not talking to me. I was sitting a little to one side when I noticed him seize hold of Mister Booker."

It didn't seem that anyone was impressed by Brown's display of temper, least of all Booker, who had some choice words for Brown when he finally released him. Everyone knew Brown was a hothead; no need to prove it.

As much as he had to say, Brown never discussed the woman's murder with his friends. Some things are best left locked away. He described only the confrontation out by the well, and that was enough to leave a lasting impression of the meeting at Sandy Cross that those attending would never forget.

Having let off some steam, Brown left for home. Little did he know that the same afternoon he was so confidently bragging to his friends, the search for Nellie by her family was about to come to a chilling end.

———•———

CHAPTER 2

Crawfordville, Georgia
March 21, 1883

I AM NOT A CRIME reporter. I do not haunt the police stations, jails and courthouses looking for my latest byline. If you are a reader of the *National Herald,* then I'm sure you've seen my name—Timothy Wood— even a time or two on the front page. My nose is usually sniffing out political news. I personally like the give and take—and underhanded dealings. Sometimes though, politics crosses the line into crime. But crime for crime's sake? No, no interest here.

But when my editors talked to me about a near 20-year-old murder case that had a serious political turn or two to it, my interest was piqued. My 30 years of deadline writing experience taught me never to dismiss an editor's suggestion outright. However, when they told me I would be going to Taliaferro County—specifically Crawfordville, Georgia—to dig up the story, my first thought was, "Which editor had I offended?"

The town of Crawfordville, I am told, is not much more than a backwater stop on the Georgia Railroad between Atlanta and Augusta. It was created about 60 years ago, when the newly formed Taliaferro County needed a county seat. The town's namesake is William Crawford, who distinguished himself in service to Presidents Madison and Monroe and ran a failed campaign for governor of Georgia. You have to wonder who Crawford upset that they would name this small village in the middle of nowhere for him.

Probably the most famous product of these parts was Alexander H. Stephens, a country lawyer who represented the area in Congress, opposed succession and went on to be elected Vice President of the Confederacy. More recently he was serving his first term as governor when he up and died just a couple of weeks ago. From my perspective, revisiting Stephens' disagreements with Confederate President Jeff Davis might be more interesting to my readers than a 20-year-old murder in a land it seems even the Lord forgot.

But timing is everything, both in life and in the newspaper business.

My editors told me Alexander Stephens' name came up in some curious ways in this murder case. So did the names of a governor and a President of the United States. How was that? I would have to find the answers for myself. There was not a lot of research available to me. Most of the people directly involved were already dead. I did find a former Union soldier, a provost marshal, to interview. I think at least those notes may come in handy.

So, on a crisp spring morning with a little preparation, I found myself in a railroad passenger car on a train pulling into the station in Crawfordville.

The ride from Atlanta was uneventful. The scenery, though, belied the fear and violence that gripped the people of this region just a handful of years ago when our nation was at war with itself. Railroad tracks wound their way from Atlanta down through the lush green forests of the piedmont to newly plowed fields of dirt, sand and red clay attended to by a new class of Georgia citizens, the freedmen.

Stepping off the train and onto the platform, leather travel bag in hand, I was amazed that Crawfordville immediately lived up to my preconceptions. On the walk from the small red-painted one-room train station down the dusty main street to the hotel, I passed through the center of government and commerce—a two-story red brick courthouse with its tree-lined square; a couple of drab mercantile shops; a feed store whose painted sign had faded many harvests ago; white clapboard churches; and, yes, a bank building with a handsome stone façade, a sure sign of prosperity. Only a few horses, wagons and a smattering of people were to be found. Most people, I would learn, were farmers, the kind of folks who didn't have a lot of time to spend in town.

My base of operations while here would be the drab gray Planters Hotel. In fact, it was the only hotel in town. At two stories high, it was a virtual skyscraper in this rather small village. At the rear of the hotel was the entrance to the local tavern. I would quickly learn it was the only place to get something to eat, unless you were cooking at home, of course. But, more importantly, the tavern was where the locals gathered to share the news of the day.

Every story needs a good source, and mine was someone who knew "Alec" Stephens, as the locals called him, better than most: his nephew Josiah. Josiah started law clerking for Alec when he finished Franklin College just before the war. Every piece of paper, every request for a meeting, every letter and every petition that came through the law office passed through Josiah's hands. He was also privy to many important conversations between "Uncle Alec" and important people. He'd been kind enough to review his uncle's files for me in anticipation of my visit.

The walk from the hotel to the Stephens' home was not a long one at all. The striking white wood-frame Crawfordville Baptist Church across the railroad tracks was a good starting point. From there, sitting on the rise beyond was Liberty Hall, the Stephens' plantation house, surrounded by all manner of outbuildings.

The setting was fit for a man of power and influence. After the war, Stephens had the house rebuilt to be a showplace. The two-story whitewashed structure with green shutters and a shiny tin roof was encased by an expansive porch that wrapped around the front and sides. Chirping birds and the whistle of the breeze through the tall pines greeted me on my walk up to the gray-painted front steps.

"Come in. Yes, come in, please." An extended hand and a welcome smile continued my friendly greeting.

"Welcome to Liberty Hall. I'm Josiah Stephens. This your first visit to our county?"

"Yes, it is, Josiah. I'm pleased to be here—and thank you for your gracious hospitality." I engaged with an outstretched hand and exchanged salutations. "I am…."

My greeter interrupted. "Yes, Mister Wood, I know very well who you are. I have been expecting you for several weeks now, but I realize Uncle Alec's late illness made an earlier engagement impossible." Then he continued with a smile, as I climbed the steps to the front porch. "Anyhow, you are now here, and I'll bet you a tall, cool drink that you can't pronounce the name of our county correctly. It is spelled T-a-l-i-a-f-e-r-r-o. Go on, Mister Wood, take a guess."

"Okay. I'll have a go at it. *Tallyaferro*? No?"

Stephens shook his head.

I tried again. "One more. *Tuleeuhferro*? If that's not right, I give up."

Josiah chuckled and said, "Take heart. Nobody guesses right. It's *Tolliver*. The county is named after a colonel from the American Revolution who pronounced his name that way."

"You sure got me with that one. Never would have guessed. Things are not always as they seem, and that's the reason I'm here…in Tolliver County. I'm just sorry I was not able to meet with your uncle personally, God rest his soul."

"The loss is definitely his." Josiah offered. "He loved this home and enjoyed sharing it with others. Many times, folks would stop in for a meal—even complete strangers." Josiah gestured toward the sky blue painted ceiling. "Got a room upstairs the family always referred to as Tramps' Room. That's where the guests would stay. More than likely though, you'd find Robert Toombs resting there. He and uncle were great friends."

"Yes," I responded. "It is quite a handsome home and grounds from what I can see. I can understand why your uncle preferred to spend his time here over Washington City and Richmond."

I was using the opportunity of this small talk to size up my host. He was short of stature, like his uncle, but much more rotund, requiring suspenders to hold up his green-and-white striped britches. Clearly Josiah had not missed many meals or opportunities for seconds. For a man in his early 40s, he had prematurely gray hair that was making a hasty retreat from his forehead. His wire-rimmed spectacles accentuated his round, and usually smiling, face. And his features shined with that reddish glow of a person who enjoyed his liquor.

But it was Josiah's manner of speech that had already drawn me in. A Southern drawl unlike any I had heard before. Slow, clear, deliberate, stately. A man in command of his language. Just a delight, I thought to myself, to hear him speak. And over the next few days, I anticipated a lot of speaking.

"This is quite a restful place," Josiah continued, "even though it is a working farm. During the war the family had thirty-one slaves living here." Josiah raised his arm in a sweeping motion across the horizon. "Uncle always took good care of the coloreds, too, because they took good care of the family."

Josiah turned to open the large front door, adorned with a brass bald eagle knocker and handle. "Please, Mister Wood, let's go inside and have a drink. I know you're tired from the train ride from Atlanta." He gestured for me to walk in, but I preferred to follow him, unsure of what might lay ahead.

Just inside the front door to the right of a spacious entryway with its ascending staircase was the parlor, a room filled with many family mementoes—pictures of Alec's half-brother Linton, someone he was closer to than anyone else, and other family members and acquaintances, including his dear friend Robert Toombs. Paintings of golden landscapes and fiery sunsets adorned the walls, along with portraits of Alec's late parents. Pens, ash trays and souvenirs from his days in Washington and Richmond were strewn about. Most significant, perhaps, was the rolling chair Alec Stephens had used in his later years.

In the middle of the room on a small table surrounded by four massive leather chairs were a pitcher of water and a pair of drinking glasses.

As I took a seat, Josiah offered a drink that had much more vigor than a simple glass of spring water. "Perhaps, later," I replied. "The water is fine for now." He poured me a glass and I took a sip.

"The finest water this side of the Fall Line, it is." Josiah took a seat opposite me. "I know why you are here, Mister Wood." His ample frame filling his chair. "And, it is not to sample the water of Liberty Hall Plantation."

"You're right." I went straight to the matter at hand. "My newspaper, the *National Herald*, is most interested in that affair in Raytown that involved your uncle." I guess "affair" was a polite way to put it. Southerners do like to put things in polite ways, bless their hearts.

"I started going through Uncle Alec's papers when you first reached out to me," Josiah said. "I was clerking for him at the time he came back home on his parole from Fort Warren in October 1865. And, since I was living here at the time, I'm very familiar with that 'affair,' myself."

Josiah paused and, lowering his glasses to the tip of his nose, peered over the frames and leaned forward toward me. "Are you sure you wouldn't want something a little stronger to drink? We make it right here in a distillery on the property."

"Maybe later," I replied. I got back to business. "I'm really puzzled about Mister Stephens' involvement. He didn't seem to have a professional relationship with any of the parties."

"In a small town, some relations are more professional than others… just like in politics," Josiah replied. "After five months in federal custody, Uncle came home wanting to be relevant again. He believed he still had a lot to offer this state he so loved. He still had lots of friends here, and it didn't take long for his law practice to develop a brisk business."

"Yes," I acknowledged, nodding my head. "But he didn't represent any of these people."

"Well, not in the eyes of the law," Josiah mused. "There are many ways to represent people, you have to understand."

"That's what I'm getting at. And I hope you'll share those details with me." I reached into my coat pocket to pull out some yellow note paper and a black pencil.

"Mister Wood, I believe I can help you," Josiah said, with a large smile erupting on his face.

I felt that I was going to be in for a long day, now that Josiah had gotten warmed up. I offered him my empty water glass and announced, "I best now take you up on that offer for some of your homebrew."

"Let's go out on the porch," Josiah said. "The breeze that comes up from below the rise will make the warmth of the day more tolerable."

———◆———

The view from a rocking chair on the front porch of Liberty Hall is truly spectacular—and inspiring. The lush green grounds bordered by tall pines and hardwoods fall away from the house down the long expanse to the railroad tracks below. Peeking from beyond the railroad tracks are the courthouse tower and the village of Crawfordville. Even in the prime of the workday, the atmosphere is serene and inviting. The sense of nature being so close—the birds, the squirrels and other odd creatures—is never lost on a visitor. Nor are the mosquitoes. Stephens' plantation was at that time just a small piece of what it once was. When emancipation came, he divided the property up among his former slaves.

"Uncle came to this property later in life. He actually grew up in Raytown after his mother and father died. The Griers, our kinfolk out there, took him in." Josiah and I had slipped into a couple of the large white rocking chairs that lined the porch, glasses of homebrew in our hands, as the story began to unfold.

"Raytown was the place to go for the moneyed folks. They'd come down from Washington, Wrightsboro, all the towns around here to enjoy fellowship at the Little River."

I injected, "It didn't hurt that the railroad put in a line to Washington through Raytown."

"No, not at all," he replied. "Growing up there, Uncle met a lot of folks. Made some lifetime friends. The Reese family among them. William and Frances were a great couple. Of course, if something happened in Raytown, quite naturally he would take an interest."

Josiah stopped the conversation long enough to take another sip and to wipe away the sweat that was beading up on his forehead. "That eastern part of Taliaferro County is good farmland, and some impressive plantations were carved out of the land. Large farms of hundreds of acres and even larger ones of thousands of acres. Up northwest of Raytown on Harden's Creek toward Washington was the Overton farm. Almost sixteen hundred acres, it was."

Josiah paused for another sip. I enjoyed one too, as I rocked my chair and took notes.

"The Overton family fell on hard times when Gilchrist Overton died. So William Gilchrist, his executor, put the farm up for sale at public auction. And on January 1, 1861, Reverend Thomas B. West of Columbia County, who pastored the Ebenezer Baptist Church, bought the place for almost fourteen thousand dollars, as I recall."

"Who was John M. Brown?" I asked, referring to some notes on the case I had brought with me.

"Well, West was a preacher, not a farmer. And you can't have a farm and work thirty-two slaves without an overseer. West brought Brown in to run the place. He had a reputation for running a tight operation and turning a handsome profit for the owner."

Josiah seemed a bit tentative. Then abruptly he changed his tone. "Hell, I'll just say it. John Brown was mean as an agitated rattlesnake. Treated his help horribly. He could not understand in his mind how a negro would work without a good whipping. And I suspect he's burning in hell today for the way he treated them."

"That's quite an indictment," I replied.

"Well, it's the truth!" He abruptly stopped his chair in the middle of a rocking movement. "He's the reason we had all this trouble. It all started because of John Brown."

"And Christopher Columbus Reese. You just mentioned his parents' names. Tell me about him." I was going down my list of key players in this crime.

Josiah resumed his rocking—and his sipping. "Christopher is quite a different story. He and his five brothers and sisters grew up on their parents' farm here in Taliaferro County. Nothing but trouble since day one for his parents. The best thing to happen to him, or so we thought, was when he signed on with the Confederate Cavalry. Wasn't but seventeen years old, but we figured the discipline would be good for him."

"It usually is for young folks," I observed. "What's the connection between Brown and Reese? Did Reese work for him?" I leaned a bit toward Josiah, not wanting to miss a word of what he was saying.

"Reese may have done some work on the plantation. But it didn't hurt that he was sweet on Brown's stepdaughter, Caroline. Gave him a good excuse to visit."

"He was probably familiar with the colored help on the farm?"

"Probably."

"And was at least familiar with Nellie West, one of the freedwomen?"

"No doubt after the events of that summer morning."

"And what," I asked, "do we know about her?

Josiah said he knew only what he had heard because slaves were not a topic of great interest among white folks. "She was about 40, maybe 50 years old. Small woman, and crippled. Bum leg. Had some kids. She was one of the house negroes, those who worked inside. Mostly worked for the mistress of the house, Sara Brown."

"Was there reason to kill her?" I asked.

"You'll find out soon enough," replied Josiah. "She was someone who over time learned to use her words to fight against those things she thought was wrong. And maybe she just got a little too uppity, as they say, for her own good."

"Uppity?" I inquired.

"On a plantation, there is a place for everyone, and everyone in their place. Need I say more?" I nodded that I understood what he was saying.

"Brown was particularly worried the help would say bad things about him to the Yankees, so he did all he could to discourage them. Tell them the Yankees would use them like pack mules—whatever would frighten them. But Nellie would not be frightened."

"You were here that summer," I reminded Josiah. "Did you hear anything about the events on July 13th on the West Plantation?" Nothing beats an eyewitness description. I wanted to know everything Josiah knew.

"Can't say I have any firsthand knowledge, and those folks who do are all dead now, even Uncle. But he and I talked about it more than once," Josiah continued as he took another sip and lit a cigar. "And, after reviewing his files for you, I suspect I know as much as anyone else does now. This goes back almost twenty years!"

I appreciated that he took my inquiry seriously. He refilled my now-empty glass and continued.

"You have to remember that times were hard. The summer of 1865 saw a general crop failure because of bad weather. Help was hard to find because many of the freemen left the farms for the towns. The Freedmen's Bureau tried to manage a free labor system to get the workers back onto their plantations. They had some success, like at the West plantation.

"It was just not a great time to be a farmer," he emphasized. "Heck, just a month after the murder, Tom West sold the entire operation to Josephus Hillsman over in Warren County for only forty-eight hundred dollars! Damndest thing. But then it's hard to run a farm when your overseer is in jail, workers are leaving and Mother Nature is on a break."

"Bet that got folks talking, for sure," I reacted.

"Not only did the farmers have it bad. Fighting was over, but the Union Army was still rounding up Southern loyalists, closing unfriendly newspapers, banning public meetings. The economy was in shambles. People who were rich one day were poor and homeless the next. Cash money was almost nonexistent. And Confederate notes? You could use them for kindling."

He was absolutely correct. The end of the war had brought desperate times on the South and the people who lived here. It didn't help that the President and Congress had come to blows over how to treat Southerners in this period they called "Reconstruction." President Johnson wanted the states to rebuild themselves, but Congress preferred a heavy hand of federal oversight. I remembered very well covering that debate. One of the lessons I learned was that if there is ever a price to be paid after fighting, it's always the losing side that pays it.

Josiah reached over and refilled my glass. Then a broad grin spread across his face. He leaned back into his chair, his head tilted back. Eyes closed. Lips pursed. I could feel a story coming on.

Then I heard him snoring.

CHAPTER 3

Crawfordville, Georgia
March 21, 1883

I DON'T KNOW WHAT ROUSED him, but following a couple of loud snorting sounds, Josiah's eyes started blinking rapidly. He quickly sat up in his chair and looked over toward me with a slight grin. Then, without missing a beat, he continued my lesson.

Josiah mentioned that townsfolk had hoped military service would be good for young Christopher Reese, or Lum, or C.C., among the names he was known by growing up in Raytown.

"In what way?" I asked.

"He'd been nothing but trouble to his parents. William and Frances were such good people. A well-respected farming family. Yes, that's what they were. He was a tall, good-looking young man with the tough frame of someone who worked with his hands on a farm. And he could fix anything. Smart kid. Would seem to be a good catch for the right lady, but, oh, Christopher was ever the restless one."

Josiah leaned in toward me. "Always looking for trouble. He'd rather have you believe trouble was looking for him. But no, truth be told, he and trouble were on a first-name basis."

"Trouble?" I thought to myself. "Tell me more," I urged. Josiah was leaning back in his rocker, black boots now propped up on the railing, no matter the scuff marks. He took a long drag from his cigar and flicked the gray ashes into a small bowl.

"He was not into pranks that other kids might play. Naw, he hung out with older boys—the boys the sheriff would soon have a professional relationship with, you know. Nothing but trouble, they were. Thieving mostly. Fighting. Taunting the negroes. There was that time Mister Kendrick's barn burned down. Hardly a timber left standing. One big pile of charcoal. He claimed he thought he saw those boys running away from the fire. But without evidence better than Mister Kendrick's 'thoughts,' the sheriff couldn't do anything about it."

Josiah put his feet down on the porch and leaned across the arm of his chair toward me.

"What probably was the tipping point came in the summer of 1863. The war was well under way, and the older boys C.C. hung with were mostly gone to the fight. Now C.C. was about 17 at the time. He had his eye on this horse over at the Campbell place. Tall, bigger than most, sleek black hair, fiery eyes, long flowing mane and tail. Looked like a horse nobility would be astride. Old man Campbell didn't want to part with the horse, but C.C. was determined to have it. Don't rightly know the circumstances, but C.C.'s dad found that fine horse in his barn one morning. Tied up in a stall, just chomping away on some hay, it was.

"Now, daddy Reese is as solid as they come. It flew all over him that Campbell's horse was in his barn. He had no doubt his son was behind the deed. And that was the point when William finally turned the tables on that boy. He trotted his son and the horse over to Campbell's place and made the boy apologize. Right there on the spot. Given anything to see that. The next thing William did was take his boy into town, right here in Crawfordville, to see Captain Beazley, who was recruiting for the Confederate military."

"That was a drastic action, if I must say," I offered.

"So, on August 1, 1863, Christopher Columbus Reese was signed up for the cavalry, where he'd see all the horses he ever wanted to see. His dad was proud that his son was supporting the South in the war, but more importantly, he thought this enlistment would knock some sense into the boy. Frances, though, worried herself unceasingly about her son getting hurt by a Yankee sharpshooter."

"Did the military service have the desired effect?" I asked, taking another sip of Josiah's famous homebrew.

"Not immediately. It didn't take long for Christopher's wicked ways to catch up with him. Four months into his enlistment, he was arrested and transferred out of the conscript camp. No one ever talked about what he did to deserve that. I suspect he got into a few too many disagreements and someone finally put him in his place—knocked some sense into him.

"Well, after a few weeks, he got shipped back to his unit and went off to run the Yankees out of North Carolina and Virginia. I'm sure the sight of him in that gray uniform waving his shiny steel sword sent tremors throughout the countryside. His unit was known as Claiborne's Partisan Rangers on account of their commanders were named Claiborne. The boys saw lots of action"—Josiah counted on his fingers as he ticked off the campaigns—"at Rodman's Point, Reed's Ferry, Quaker Bridge, New Bern, Swift Creek, the Bermuda Hundred front. From what we know, Reese acquitted himself very well by staying out of further trouble and avoiding stray Yankee shots.

"But, just a year into his enlistment, in the summer of 1864, the Confederate government made the decision to disband the rangers. No matter that their reputation was instilling fear in the minds of the blue coats, the military brains in Richmond sent the boys back to their homes in Georgia and North Carolina to muster in with their state guards. Christopher, though, had seen enough military life and returned to Raytown."

I was writing notes as fast as Josiah could spin his yarn. Keeping up wasn't easy, but the story was quite interesting so far. I asked how he turned out when he returned home.

"He spent the rest of the war helping on the family farm, working in the fields and helping around the house. His folks were real pleased with his new attitude. But the demons were still at work in him. When he wasn't tilling a field, you'd find him mouthing off at someone in the tavern over there behind the hotel here in Crawfordville. Or trying to find a way to see Miss Caroline, John Brown's stepdaughter. She was a couple years older than Reese, but that didn't matter to him. He found those curly golden locks and her slim figure quite irresistible, what he wanted. And, just like with Campbell's horse, he was going to do whatever it would take to have her."

"Caroline was living with the Browns?" I asked.

"Quite a bunch of them in that house—Caroline, her mom, step-father and six siblings—a house full. Yes, indeed." Josiah showed no signs of slowing down. The story was rolling off his lips, so long as he kept them moist with that corn liquor. "Brown, he was born in South Carolina in the late twenties, I recall. Sarah was much older than he was when they married, and she already had a couple of kids of her own—Caroline and her brother Jimmy, who was also an overseer. The West farm is not a place that we know much about. Brown and his family kept to themselves out on the property. Occasionally, the women would come into town. You'd see them shopping."

"Did the war change anything on the farm?" I stood up to take off my brown traveling jacket and loosen the collar on my bright blue plaid shirt. The day was beginning to warm up nicely.

"Even after the war ended, the Browns kept to themselves, and so did their coloreds. In slavery days, a negro could get a pass to visit relatives on other farms, or they might accompany the overseer to town for shopping, but not Brown's darkies. To see any of them, you had to go to the farm. As a result, the plantation was not something folks paid much mind to. You know, if you don't see something, you don't think about it."

"Josiah, do you know anything about where Brown came from?"

"Tom West brought him to Raytown from a farm in South Georgia where he was overseer. As I said, the family mostly stayed out on the farm. But Brown would show up for drinks with the guys at a friend's house or the tavern, or join a squirrel hunt or fishing outing. Sandy Cross was the place the men mostly liked to gather."

"Even isolated on the farm, the negroes still were able to learn what life was like for the freedmen?"

"The negroes would talk, sure enough," Josiah said. "They have a way of passing information around that rivals Western Union! And they had plenty to say about plantation life under John Brown. You see, the overseer was not expected to work the crop but was expected to be with the hands constantly. With the pressure they were under from the owners to work the slaves and produce a crop, it was a job best suited for men who were naturally cruel.

"So, no," Josiah continued, "I wasn't surprised when I heard Brown had been arrested for killing Nellie. Nope. Not surprised one bit. The darkies had been saying for some time that there was bad blood between the two of them. Some said he treated her worse than the others. Even after emancipation, the negroes say, she was treated like a slave.

"Tales of brutality on the West farm were widely known, especially during the war years. Folks came to understand that such talk was better left alone, even by white folks. Oh, but what stories could be told…."

———◆———

West Plantation
Raytown, Georgia
Spring 1865
The end of four years of fighting seemed for many to open the door to a joyous new era. For the whites that meant the boys were coming home from the front, and their families would at last be reunited. For the negroes, the end of the fighting would bring freedom, but in their insular world, they had no concept of how things would change for them in a free society. The looming uncertainty had the help quite worried.

Tom West's plantation in Raytown is isolated from the rest of the world. It is so large, it is a world unto itself, extending over 1,500 acres from Harden's Creek on the south to up along the railroad line toward Washington, about nine miles to the north. A constellation of buildings—including the cook house, barn, slave quarters, hen house and many more structures—surrounds the main house where the overseer's family lives.

West's acreage is broken up into several fields that were best known by the activity in each. High on a rise overlooking the cluster of buildings is the corn field that is as busy as a colony of pollen-hunting bees in the spring. From near sunup to the advance of darkness, the sounds of the negroes are heard as they toil to get the ground plowed and prepared for seeding, then nurture their seedlings on to the harvest that will follow. Short-staple cotton with its growing season of about 200 days is well suited for Wilkes County's rich dirt, as are feed corn and red oats.

Farming is hard work, especially under the heat of an oppressive Georgia sun, the relentless strangling humidity, and those pesky mosquitos and gnats. For the slaves, the farm was their life's work. They adapted to the climate but seemed not so adapted at times to plantation discipline. Overseers kept them in line with frequent beatings, which were meant to be corrective actions for misbehavior, but more often were a way for the overseer to let off some steam. The coloreds lived in constant fear of the sting of their master's whip.

The slaves kept within their own social order. House slaves were superior to those who worked the fields. Well into middle age, Nellie West was past her prime for field work. She was one of the house slaves, doing the washing and spinning for John Brown's family. So she was a daily fixture in the yard outside the wash house, hanging wet clothes on the white cotton clothes line strung between two poles.

Washing and spinning were skills Nellie learned at an early age from other house servants, under the watchful eye of the lady of the house. As a spinner she had access to her master's fine quality cloth and linens from which she would make clothing and quilts and other textile items that allowed her artistic abilities to soar. Muslin, lace, velvet and brightly colored silk were the tools of Nellie's trade. However, for a negro woman, these creations were merely objects to be admired, to be worn only by the mistress of the manor. Nellie's own clothes were made of coarse, colorless cotton—negro cloth, they called it.

The women spent evenings in their cabins in the quarters spinning and weaving, lulled by the serenity of the spinning wheel's unique whirring sound. They also dyed some of the cloth blue using the indigo they grew for the color, or used bark and leaves to make the tan and brown colors of a hickory-colored stripe pattern.

Nellie was close to her family, all of whom adopted the last name of their owner Tom West. "Family" had a broad definition in the slave culture extending to far beyond a mother, father and children. Nellie's family included her four children: Raphael, her son who was known as Rafe; her other son, Gabrel; and her daughters, Kitty and Lucinda. Also living in the quarters were her brother Elleck and his wife Millie, and her brother Sam and his wife Caroline. Another half dozen others claimed some form of family relations, either real or imagined. As close as they were, Nellie knew that in slavery, any one of them could be sold off as the owner's property at any time. She was fortunate that so many of her kinfolk lived on the same plantation because splitting families was common.

Many of the slave owners in this part of Georgia allowed liberal visitations among their slave populations. The negroes used their passes to create their own community activities including inter-plantation dances, corn-shuckings, cotton picking competitions, religious activities and harvest festivals.

Not so for the slaves watched over by John Brown, who preferred a practice that was more common to plantations on the coastal plain. He, in effect, isolated Tom West's slaves, fearing they might organize an insurrection if allowed to communicate with those on other farms.

For the West slaves, the farm was not only their community; it was their 1,500-acre world. And John Brown was the supreme ruler.

The slave quarters provided the West negroes respite from the day's work and a place of safe harbor and refuge from the whip where they could mingle among themselves, free from the prying eyes of the overseer. This community was a cluster of drab, weathered one- and two-room cabins away from the main house, yet close enough to be observed. The cabins, some made from logs and others from planks, were all lined up in a double row facing each other with a generous growth of mulberry trees to provide shade. Each home had a small garden for subsistence farming and a chicken yard.

The cabins in the quarters were sparsely furnished with dirt floors. Nellie and the others didn't have much to call their own. She had one bed with a mattress of straw and corn shucks, a bench and a chair. The children slept on the floor. Cooking was done on the stone fireplace in the house, and the food was usually eaten outside on tin plates. In the absence of the comforts her master enjoyed, Nellie was left to treasure her family—and her faith.

Traveling preachers, called "Chairbacks," showed in the quarters in the evening to bring the message of salvation. Praise meetings, usually held in a cabin or out under the trees, were special moments of emotional preaching and soulful praying.

Nellie and the family always looked forward to Sunday as a day off for everyone. To get ready, the farm would bustle with activity Fridays and Saturdays when all the cooking was done for the Sabbath. White and colored together would all go to church. They loaded the wagons otherwise used to haul crops and farm tools and attended the nearest house of worship.

Discipline in a white church was serious business. Negroes sat segregated in the gallery. No one dared do anything to disrespect or embarrass their masters. There was no looking around in church. No looking to the right or to the left, no matter what happened. You couldn't even halfway smile; that was particularly hard when listening to those tiresome sermons. They tell the story of the time Reverend Amason was preaching at the Methodist Church, and a dog ran up into the crawl space under the building. Every time Amason belted out something, the dog would commence to barking. "Woof. Woof. Woof." But no one so much as snickered.

One of the places where Nellie found the hope of a better life for her and her family was in music. Usually someone with a fiddle got a tune going, and the crowd joined in to sing along and dance. All the songs had a message, with many songs crafted from the personal experiences of the sorrow found in another day in bondage.

"Poor Nellie, poor girl
Poor Nellie, poor girl
Poooorr Neelliiee, pooooorr Neelliiee,
Heaven shall be my home."

One spring morning Nellie's sister-in-law Millie, sporting a large straw hat to keep off the sun, was in the garden with some of the other women of the West family putting out greens. The garden was an important part of the food chain on the plantation. Items grown there—potatoes, peas, beans, squash, cabbage—all contributed to the farm's self-sufficiency.

The sound of a slamming door startled the women enough to end their chattering abruptly. Nellie briskly came walking out of the house, and all heads pivoted in her direction. They knew she should be inside spinning, far removed from the yard. But there she went, walking past them without so much as a word. She headed down around the main house and on behind the hen house.

"Nellie West!" came the shout that shattered the restored calmness of the scene. Even from outside, there was no mistaking the voice of overseer Brown, as he shouted the name of their matriarch from inside the house. He burst through the door like a thrashing, charging bull.

His left hand was balled into a fist, punching into the air. In the sure grip of his swinging right hand, a bunch of green willow switches cut through the air.

Brown continued to shout Nellie's name as he followed her path across the yard, down behind the house and to the hen house. Not once did Brown look over in the direction of the West women tending the garden. Like a hunter, he was too focused on his prey.

"I's got a bad feelin'," Millie said to herself. She had been many times a witness to an all-too-familiar scene on the farm since Brown's arrival about five years earlier.

Then came the cries. High-pitched screams. Oh, so mournful a sound. The sound of those switches swishing through the air. The slap of fresh wood against bare skin. Nellie's painful cries piercing the air. The women in the garden were looking off toward the hen house but unable to see what was going on. However, Millie knew exactly what was happening.

"He's whipping her mighty bad today," Millie shared with the others. "Right smart," another observed.

Down behind the hen house, Nellie had been stripped of every bit of clothing. Her flowered yellow dress—one of her favorites—and the colorful handkerchief she wore around her neck to catch her sweat were both in a pile on the ground next to her. Her small frame stood stark naked, trembling as her body recoiled with every new strike by the willow switches clutched in Brown's right hand. The thrashing continued until Nellie could stand no more. She finally collapsed into a ball of black, bleeding flesh.

Nellie was one of Brown's favorite targets for his scorn. At times he would pull Nellie up out of her spinning chair, drag her behind the hen house and lash into her naked flesh. In addition to painful switches, Brown also used a black leather-handled whip with trailing bloody rawhide on one end.

"God damn you," he would shout in a voice so loud that no one could miss the message. "If you fool with me, I will whip you to death!" And no one who heard him doubted him. The slaves believed he would kill every last one of them, given the chance.

When Brown again came into sight while rounding the hen house, sending chickens scurrying for cover, the girls scrambled from the garden to retrieve Nellie's scarred body—and her clothing. They took her to her small log house in the quarters. A homemade salve applied to her back eased the pain that seized her as each cut was addressed. There would be no more washing and spinning for Nellie for the rest of this day.

On the West farm the tide did not turn when the war ended. Brown continued to treat the negroes as if they were in bondage. They were trapped in a system that offered them freedom but put a premium on keeping them on their farms to continue working. They would be paid in a portion of the crops they raised, or they could be paid in wages set by the Freedmen's Bureau: $7 a month for male field hands and $6 a month for women. House servants would make a couple dollars more.

Brown's brutality knew no limits. Once Nellie's brother Sam became a free man, he made the mistake of taking off for Washington to complain to the provost marshal about Brown's continued brutal treatment of the workers. In the plantation society, the slaves would report abusive overseers to their owners. But with this new thing called freedom, Sam now looked on the Union government as his protector—not Tom West. That was a big mistake.

Once back on the farm, Sam and some of the other negroes went to laying their corn crop in the middle of a warm spring afternoon. Sam was no doubt using this time in the field to share with the others the details of his meeting with the Union soldiers, hoping that his actions would lead to a better life for all of them. Their hope, however, turned out to be nothing more than foolish dreaming. Expectations were shattered when Brown arrived in the field to confront Sam. He knew what Sam had done and did not like being crossed one bit.

Brown dismounted his horse and called to Sam's nephew, young William. He said, "Boy, fetch me some switches from that ash." The other workers stood in amazement. What was going on, they all wondered. Surely working the field was not cause for alarm.

"Sam," Brown commanded as he turned toward Sam's now-quivering body.

Immediately, Sam knew what was unfolding. He had been punished before, but this time Brown was especially agitated. "Take off your shirt and drop your britches." A big man with a tender heart, Sam was the one the younger negroes looked up to. He was a man of principle and courage, but the sting of the master's whip would hurt him no less than it hurt the others.

Silently and submissively Sam stood there in the field in front of the others, shirt off and pants down, the afternoon sun reflecting off his sweaty dark brown skin. Brown abruptly pulled his silver pistol from his belt, raised it high and, with a quick downward stroke, smacked the butt against the side of Sam's head, sending Sam's straw hat sailing through the air. The loud cracking sound that followed startled them all. But such was the fear they had for Brown that they stood motionless, afraid to move to offer any help.

Sam wobbled a bit but remained on his feet. Blood seeped from the cut the gun butt had opened on his head and also trailed down his bare chest. Not a sound came from his lips. His eyes began to water as his face drew itself into a contorted grimace.

Then without another word, Brown used a tan handkerchief to wipe the blood from the white bone grips on the pistol and slipped the gun back into his belt. But Brown had more for his victim. He tightened his right fist and with a loud thud jabbed it hard into Sam's face, sending his head spinning. Sam was stunned and let out a mournfully loud moan. The other negroes shared glances among themselves but remained still. Sam's knees began to wobble and he struggled to remain standing.

Brown then thrust his fingers into Sam's mouth, jerking and pulling from one side to the other.

When William finally ran up with the switches, he was shocked at what he saw. His big, strong uncle—face reddened, head bleeding— barely able to stand. That would be enough punishment for any man, but Brown was far from finished. He grabbed the fresh green switches from William's hand and pushed the boy back with the others.

Brown turned back toward Sam and shouted, "Get down on the ground, boy!" He held the switches tightly in his right hand and tapped them into his left hand.

"Face down!" Brown grabbed Sam's feet and pulled them away from his torso.

"Arms out!" Sam quickly responded, but not fast enough for Brown, who kicked him hard in his side with the steel tip of his boot.

With the switches still firmly gripped in his right hand, Brown let loose on Sam's bare back and bottom. Brown thrashed wildly at the helpless Sam. His long brown hair danced in the air as Brown bobbed up and down, raking the sticks of wood back and forth across the ex- posed skin of his helpless prey. The slapping sound of the switches cut- ting into Sam's body was unforgettable. Sam cried out from the searing pain, asking the Lord to have mercy.

"Damn the Lord," Brown responded. "He can't do a thing for you, boy." In fact nobody could to anything for Sam. None of the other ne- groes dared to do anything to interfere, lest they be whipped next.

"Let this be a lesson for crossing me."

This was a lesson Sam would never forget. Neither would William nor the other negroes working with Sam in the field that day. Finishing the deed, Brown tossed the now blood-red sticks aside and splashed a bucket of salty water on Sam's blistered skin. He then mounted his chest- nut mare and rode back toward the main house.

One of the field hands had run to collect Caroline West to fetch her beaten and bloodied husband back to their cabin, where she could tend to his wounds. She knew what to do, because she had done it so many times for Sam and others—cleaning the wounds, applying the salve. In the coming weeks the cuts and blisters would heal, but the scars would be a constant reminder of another "lesson" taught by John Brown.

At 35, Caroline was very familiar with the manner of Brown's discipline because she, too, had felt the sting of his brutality. Her lesson had come at the end of another long, hot day under the Georgia sun.

Caroline was responsible for the daily milking of the farm's cows. Brown had given her explicit instructions about what time of day to perform that chore. And she was most sensitive to following the overseer's wishes. So one day while she was working in the field, milking time arrived. She didn't want to cross Brown by failing her milking duties, so Caroline unhitched the brown and white horse she was plowing with and rode it back to the barn.

Brown approached her in the barn, but he was not there to tell her how much he appreciated her attention to the cows. In his right hand was a cluster of several green oak switches. He was very angry that Caroline had left the field with the horse in the middle of plowing. Without a word, he grabbed her by her hair and snatched her up from the milking stool. She was shocked…and confused. In rapid succession, Brown pulled her plain white homespun dress down to her waist and proceeded to whip her across her back. "You damn bitch," he fiercely growled.

Caroline felt the thrashing of the sticks of wood against her back—sharp and stinging. Once. Twice. Again. And again. She cried out as the pain intensified. Then as abruptly has this cruel beating had begun, it was over. Another "lesson" delivered.

"Go on to the plowing," Brown instructed, "and if you don't make that horse step up, I'll take you down again." Caroline pulled her dress back up to cover her body. As the cloth made contact with her wounds, the blood soaked through, the red slashes now a visual warning to others who would cross their overseer.

Brown followed Caroline back to the field, where she hitched the horse up to the plow and resumed her work. She had not made more than one more round across the field before Brown pulled her from under the plow straps and made her lie down in the freshly tilled red clay. The others with her were astonished but helpless to respond. Those negroes in the field knew better than to involve themselves in Brown's disciplining of others, for fear he would give them an equal measure. Some watched; others went about their work. But no one could ignore the cries of pain coming from Caroline, a young woman whose striking features and light brown skin were now contorted in agony.

This time Brown had grabbed her clothes from the bottom and pulled upward. If not for a cotton string around her waist, he would have stripped her naked. Brown commenced a terrible beating of the woman, more lashes than anyone could count. He kept whipping until Caroline went into a spasm. Blood was now splattered everywhere—over her body, her dress, the dirt. Even Brown's own clothes were dotted red by blood.

The negroes watching Caroline's writhing body trembled in fear, fear not just of John Brown but of what else might be at play. They were beginning to believe that something was conjured up in the woman's body. They had heard tales of such things all their lives, and now they were faced with the real fear that some terrible creature might actually crawl out of her body.

"William," Brown commanded, looking over to one of the other negroes and pointing to Caroline's dress, "strip those clothes off her." Young William didn't want anything to do with the scene being played out before him, but he knew better. He would be next if he did not do as he was told.

He hesitatingly walked over to Caroline, who was balled up in a fetal position on the ground. William tugged and tried to pull her dress off, but the cotton string around her waist held its grip. Frustrated, Brown instead told the young boy, "Take her yonder to that puddle of water and clean her up."

William and some of the others carried Caroline to the edge of the field where a hole still held about three feet of water from recent rains.

They rolled her about in the water, much like a pig wallows in mud. Caroline was clearly not in her senses.

Sam was summoned to get her. He found her in that puddle where the others had left her. He lifted Caroline out and put his wife on the plow horse for a ride back to the quarters. Yes, Sam was a big man, but at the same time he was a helpless man against the tormentor of his family.

Now he cleaned her up the best he could and put clean clothes on her, but these actions were little consolation for the near-fatal beating she had just suffered through. In a bit, Brown's wife Sara showed up at the cabin to rub Caroline's head with N0. 6, a salve to help bring her back to her senses. Yes, Caroline survived, but only to live another day in the hell on earth the West Plantation had become.

Brown believed negroes worked only when they were sternly disciplined. It was a belief he would come to regret.

CHAPTER 4

————

Crawfordville, Georgia
March 22, 1883

"AND YOUR ACCOMMODATIONS LAST NIGHT, Mister Wood? How was the hotel?" Josiah wanted to know, as he greeted my arrival once again at Liberty Hall.

I had spent the night in about the only place to spend the night in Crawfordville, other than the city jail. The Planters Hotel was nice, but what's "nice" was relative. At least the adjacent tavern was convenient for a meal.

"The bed was soft and the room was quiet." I was trying to be polite. Southerners are very polite people, after all.

"No matter," Josiah replied. "It's not like you are moving in."

The walk up to the Stephens' house on this morning was delightful. And from our perch on the porch, we could look out to see the morning unfold before our eyes. The bright sunrise provided a silhouette for the tall brown pines and lush green legacy oaks on the horizon. It wasn't long before the steam whistle on the approaching railroad engine from Augusta signaled to everyone that the new workday had broken.

"I was looking through my notes last night," I remarked as I pulled the notepad from my coat pocket. "Just couldn't help but focus in on what life on that plantation must was like for Nellie and her family under John Brown's reign."

"Pure Hell is how I would describe it." Josiah was holding nothing back. "That's how the darkies describe it, too."

"An apt phrase," I offered.

"Pure meanness."

"Agree." But I was convinced there had to be more to it.

"Oh, yeah." Over the years Josiah had gained a bit of insight into the life of the negroes on the West plantation. "I'm told Brown even had his own whip made to dish out punishment. It was longer than a man's arm. Had a leather thong on it." He gestured with his hands to demonstrate the length. "Twelve to fourteen inches of tanned buckskin. Wide as two fingers and tapering down to a point. They showed it during the trial."

I was becoming more unsettled about what I was hearing.

"Nellie was one of his favorite targets because she would stand up to him. He didn't like that. Yeah, the negroes were all scared of him. 'If you fool with me,' he would say, 'I will whip you to death.' That's what they said he would say. And they believed him; he would do it!"

"I guess the negroes never had Ephesians read to them," I offered. "'Servants, be obedient to them that are your masters according to the flesh, with fear and trembling....'"

Josiah responded without missing a beat, "And 'ye masters, do the same things unto them, forbearing threatening.'"

I smiled. So did Josiah. Obviously, neither of us was meant to be in the pulpit Sunday.

Returning to the subject at hand, I asked, "Did Brown ever kill any of the slaves?"

"Not that I am aware of. People who knew him said he was a lot of bluster. And meanness."

"After the war ended and before Nellie was killed, how often did he punish the slaves on the West plantation?"

"Every day, or so it seemed to the negroes working for Tom West. That's how they testified at trial."

"How so?" I asked.

"After the war the Freedmen's Bureau told the negroes to stay on the farms and enter into contracts with their former owners. Some would work for pay, others for a share of the crops they grew. West's negroes were sharecroppers. Some white folks made no distinction between discipline under free labor and under slave labor. If it took a whipping to get someone to work, lay it on!"

"So, the whippings, the beatings, they continued?" I asked as I took notes.

"Yes, and Brown was one of the worst of the lot. He still believed in the old style of plantation discipline, even though the military authorities and the bureau told the farmers to stop such tactics. The darkies were told by Freedmen's Bureau agents that there would be no abuse, no selling or buying of freed slaves and no breaking up of families. But in return, they were also told they had to work. Idleness was not acceptable."

"And the West plantation appears anything but idle," I suggested.

Josiah continued, "The one place where the negroes could be themselves was their nightly praise meeting."

"Praise meeting?" I asked. "As in church?"

"The white churches were quite active in seeing to it that the darkies learned about Jesus, so their souls would be saved. It was against the law for the slaves to learn to read and write, but there always seemed to be one of them who could lay out a Bible verse or two to deliver up the Word of the Lord. Evenings they'd all gather in the quarters under the trees or in one of their shacks—some plantations even had small chapels for them to use. They'd commiserate over those among them who had been whipped that day, or were sick or something." He gestured with his arms wide open. "And of course they would sing."

My education of the South had been nothing more than a never-ending series of surprises. I believe Josiah was the best teacher I could have found.

I took my leave that afternoon to visit Raytown. The ride was not a long one at all in the horse and buggy Josiah loaned me. He would have come along, except he was still putting his late uncle's affairs in order.

Heading out to the east from Crawfordville into the bright midday sun bursting through the deep blue sky gave me a new perspective of this area. The countryside is mainly rolling hills, many showing the evidence of human labor bringing in the new crop. Rows and rows plowed into rich brown and black dirt as far as the eye could see.

Through the stillness I could hear the faint songs of the workers rising up from the fields. Their voices blending in melancholy harmonies. Perhaps these were the songs they'd sing at their praise meetings. The melodies created some of the finest, but loneliest, music I had ever heard. The words recalled hard times.

No more hundred lash for me
No more hundred lash
No more hundred lash for me
Many a thousand die.

The fear of the lash is what overseers used to keep their negroes in line.

I passed a couple of farms where the small houses were empty and boarded up, fields overgrown...testaments to good times past. The Reconstruction era was hard on most folks, especially land owners, who were now paying for help and feeling the onslaught of Union taxation. If you can't feed your family or pay your help, then how should you be expected to pay the government? Makes no matter. If your taxes aren't paid, your property is sold on the courthouse steps. Maybe a new owner will have better luck. Or, maybe he'll just leave the house to the elements, just as many farms I saw had been left in disrepair.

When the songs of the workers faded into the distance, I found the sounds of nature especially pleasing. Between the rhythmic beats of the horse's hooves on the hard red clay road, I could hear songbirds full of life, the loud calls of the mockingbirds and the crows competing for attention. It wasn't unusual to see a deer alongside the road foraging for a treat, or a gray squirrel scampering away with a delicious acorn. None of this activity was like what I saw in the city where I lived. Our trees were tall, drab buildings. Our songbirds were the clang of the trollies. Taliaferro County might not be so bad after all, I was beginning to think.

I crossed the railroad tracks that led toward the north and on to Washington, passing by the railroad station and mercantile store that comprised the hub of commerce in Raytown. Pausing for a moment, my mind wandered to the events that had happened just four miles north of here on the West farm. I would have to visit there, I thought, but not today. Time for that later. This afternoon, I was looking for people who knew John Brown. People who could tell me what kind of an overseer he had been. Josiah has described him as a "demon." Really?

Not far along the road to Wrightsboro I came upon two older men conversing across a fence. The taller one in blue coveralls wearing a ragged straw hat seemed particularly animated. His arms were waving and his body rocking to and fro. The other fellow had on green tweed pants, a bleached cotton shirt and a leather cap. He appeared totally immersed in the conversation. From the looks of their discussion, I had a feeling this was not their first meeting. I pulled the buggy up short to the side of the road to get out to introduce myself.

"Timothy Wood of the *National Herald*," I said, tipping my hat. I had picked up the straw topper earlier in Crawfordville to keep the blazing Georgia sun off my head, since much of my hair had abandoned me in the aging process. Besides, seems every man in Crawfordville has a hat of some sort, and every woman a bonnet. Don't know if wearing a hat helped me fit in, but I sure appreciated the shade it afforded on this day.

"Seaborn Acree's the name," the older of the two strangers said extending his weatherworn hand. In his frayed outfit, he looked every bit a farmer. Then it hit me.

"Mister Acree, you were a neighbor of John Brown's."

"That I was," he responded, lifting his hat and running his fingers through his gray hair. "So was S.H.," he said pointing to his companion. "Both of us knew Brown."

"Used to share tales with him at Sandy Cross." The companion extended his hand. "Perkins is my last name," said S.H., extending his hand. "But most folks call me Cotton, on account of my white hair," he said removing his cap. Like Acree, Perkins' well-tanned face gave him the appearance of someone who has spent the better part of his life in the fields.

"I heard you were in town," Acree offered. "Josiah was talking you up in the tavern last night. Said you were a newspaper man. You was sent here to dig up a story on the West Plantation murder."

"That was a long time ago," offered Perkins. "Not something we think about on a regular basis."

"Then you know I'm working on a story on that murder back in '65 involving the freedwoman, Nellie West."

"Horrible. Just horrible," offered Perkins, shaking his head side to side.

Acree looked over toward Perkins. "Cotton, I guess it's all right to talk about it, since it's all in the past."

"Yeah, the past," said Perkins. "The past. What's there…stays there."

I asked Acree to tell me if Brown ever talked about whipping the negroes.

Acree slipped his hat back to expose his forehead and wiped it with a red handkerchief he had pulled from a back pocket. "One time he had a boy sent up to him by an owner to drive his oxen. Brown whipped him, and I understood from Brown that he took his clothes off—I suppose from his waist down."

"And how did he come to tell you this?" I asked.

"The way he come to tell me about it, the boy got loose and run off. He tried to get dogs. He did not succeed; or if he got them at all, it was too late to track him." Acree looked over toward Perkins, who responded with an approving glance.

"Mister Acree, what was that about Brown taking the colored's clothes off?" I found his reference to undressing the coloreds as rather curious.

"He said his manner of discipline to whip negroes is to buck them. I do not know whether he told me so at the time. But I have heard it frequently from him."

"And you Mister Perkins? You ever hear of Brown mistreating his help?" I asked as I wrote in my notebook.

This time Perkins looked over toward Acree, who nodded his head approvingly. "Mister Wood, I have heard him speak of punishing negroes, as I believe is the custom of all masters, by the rod."

"And what about whipping them naked?" The whole concept of whipping folks with their clothes off was hard for me to grasp.

"I think I heard him say that he liked to whip them on the skin when he did correct them." Perkins was scratching his head as he tried to recall what Brown had told him. "The words are, as near as I can recollect, that he did not like to correct them, but when he did so, he wanted to whip them on the skin."

"And why did he have a need to whip them in the first place?" I asked, pressing the conversation deeper.

Perkins replied, "He said he had some very stubborn boys, and his employer was depending upon him for a crop, and that he was compelled to force those boys to work."

"Was Brown one to bluster? You know, swear at and threaten his negroes?" I asked.

"Yes," Acree shot back. "It is very common. But Mister Wood, I have never known one to be killed pursuant to such threats."

"So why threaten in the first place?" I naively inquired.

"It is done more to frighten a man," Acree replied, shifting his weight against a fence post.

"Yes," Perkins injected, nodding his head in agreement. "To frighten a man."

"A whip would be frightening enough for me, but I just don't get this business of stripping the negroes to whip them," I remarked, continuing to take notes as the men spoke.

Perkins chimed in: "He said that when he had to correct them he did not want to whip their clothing; he wanted to whip their hide."

"I heard that too, Cotton," said Acree.

"Hard to imagine such bitterness in such a beautiful setting," I said, my eyes sweeping the horizon of blue sky and puffy white clouds colliding with the lush green of the woodlands.

"Don't get me wrong," cautioned Acree. "Brown was not typical of the way our farms are run."

"No, sir," interrupted Perkins, shaking his head.

"We all had difficulties adjusting to that thing they called free labor," Acree continued.

Perkins interrupted again. "What was so 'free' about it? Nobody gave me nothing."

"Cotton, we already fought that fight." You could see Acree's frustration in his expression. Cleary, he and Perkins had had this discussion many times. "You just need to get over it."

"Don't know if I'll live that long," replied Perkins.

"Well, dammit. Try." With that, Acree took his leave to get back into his field. Perkins was not far behind.

I climbed back into the buggy and headed west for the ride back to Crawfordville.

CHAPTER 5

———◆———

West Plantation
Raytown, Georgia
Friday, July 14, 1865

WHEN NELLIE FAILED TO RETURN from Washington, her family became concerned, as you might expect. The farmhands had all been given a holiday by Brown from Thursday night until Monday as reward for getting the corn crop in from the field. This hiatus created a perfect opportunity for West's family to begin a search for the missing matriarch.

Nellie's son Rafe spent all day Friday traveling between Tom West's home in Warren County and Washington looking for his mother.

"No, Rafe. I haven't seen anything of her," said West, when Nellie's son asked of her whereabouts. It was hard to tell just how concerned West was about the missing woman, if concerned at all. After all, she was no longer his property, no longer a commodity with value. If anything, crippled and insolent negroes were now a liability.

Even so, West tried his best to be responsive to Rafe, whose tall, thin frame was draped in cast-off black pants and a red shirt. His shoes were dusted mightily by the long walk he had taken in search of his mother. The young man remembered his place on the white man's farm as a negro. He never made eye contact with West.

"Marsa Brown drive her off." You could sense the apprehension in his voice. "I just wanna find whar she at." Rafe did little to elicit any empathy from West.

"There's no reason to be uneasy about her," West coolly responded. "You'll hear from her in a few days, or see her sooner than expected."

"Well, I'm gonna hunt 'til I finds her," replied Rafe with determination in his voice.

Friday was a day the negroes usually worked the field. West was curious why one would show up at his house on a workday. "Did Brown give you a holiday?"

"Yes, suh, he shore did," responded Rafe as he took his leave. "We brung da crop in fer him yestady."

After spending the night in Washington, Rafe returned to the West plantation Saturday morning. He arrived around 11 o'clock. His Uncle Sam, Nellie's brother, informed him that Brown was away from the farm fishing. Walking back to the cabin, Rafe ran into Brown's wife.

"It's no use coming back here," Sara warned him. "Mister Brown is going to run you off." Ever the dutiful wife, Sara had little use for insolence from the negroes. She liked to strut her ample frame around the farm in the fine dresses stitched by Nellie, but she had little use otherwise for the help.

"'Cause I went off looking for momma?" Rafe asked. He never got an answer.

It wasn't long before Brown arrived at the farm with his fishing party, dragging lines of the catfish they had caught. Rafe took their horses to the barn and put up the animals without any comment from Brown. Not even an inquiry about his absent mother. Rafe spent the rest of Saturday at home, wondering what had become of his mother.

The Sunday morning sunrise came early on the farm. Not early enough, though, for the chickens, which were already cackling up a storm as they pecked about the yard. The hen house was the busiest spot on the farm at the beginning of each day. Not to be outdone, the cows noisily reminded the farmhands they were ready to head to the pasture for the day's gazing.

"You wants ta see me, suh?" Rafe asked. He had responded to Brown's summons to come to the house.

"Just where have you been?" Brown asked, as they stood by the well.

"Went ta hunt fer my mammy," Rafe replied. The lad's gaze wandered, never making eye contact with Brown.

"What do you want to hunt for your mother for?" Brown inquired.

"Wanna find out where she be," Rafe said, shifting his weight from side to side in a rocking motion. "She's old lady, not able ta takin' care of herself. I's goin' hunting for her 'til I finds her."

Brown said: "I didn't think you cared anything for her."

"Oh, Marsa Brown, I cares as much fer her as anyones else cares for their mammy, or you would for your'n. She be de only friend I got, and I feels disposed ta take care of her so long as she remains on da top o' da earth," he said, jabbing his finger toward the ground to emphasis his point.

"I had thought to drive you away, but seeing as how you came back, I'll let you stay as long as you do right." Brown's voice was firm; his words specific and calculated. "And if you want to go off, wait until Monday morning, and I will send you off."

Rafe's voice changed as a bit as even more worry crept into his demeanor. He had lost his mother, and now was he about to be kicked off the farm, separated from his family?

"Look, I's be workin' here till I had done made crop. Ain't disposed to go an' leave it. Can't make no livin' nowheres else. Too late in da year. I's bound ta stay ta Chritmus cause I don't wants ta go nowhere else," he declared.

Brown responded: "If you behave yourself, you can stay."

But things just didn't seem right with Rafe. Brown's tone changed as he told Rafe never to set foot in the farm house again. "I know what you are thinking. You believe I killed your mother, which is a thing I don't do in good times, and which I know I would never do in time of difficulty, like now.

"Now, get along, boy," Brown said dismissively.

Rafe walked back to the quarters for breakfast with his siblings and to organize everyone in a search for Nellie.

Rafe first sent out his 15-year-old brother, Gabrel, and his sisters, Kitty and Lucinda, to keep up the hunt for their mother. As he saw them off, he confided, "I think she's dead." The children did not respond.

Brown was also on the move about the farm. He caught up with Gabrel before he reached the creek.

"Where's Rafe?" Brown asked.

"He be huntin' for mammy," the boy nervously replied.

"I don't know where she is. I expect she's gone to Washington. That's what she said," Brown continued, trying to dissuade the children from their mission. "She said she was afraid the Yankees would not take her in, and she was afraid to go there. And she said she thought she would go to her master's, Mister West, but she was afraid that he would not take her in either. Then she said she was going to old Moses Butler's.

"Last I heard of her she was going along by Raytown Depot." Brown was conjuring up doubts to confuse the youngsters about where to begin their search.

"But don't you be going down and fooling around that railroad, as the cars could come along and kill you!"

Separately, two other workers, Tom and Wash, the farmhands on the pickaxe, joined Rafe to search in another direction. They walked through old pastures and looked in all the "bad places." When they got to the railroad line to Washington, they stopped for a rest.

Rafe mused to himself: "Thought fer sure she be ta Master Randolph's or in da old pasture." The three were now sitting on the railroad track, studying which way to go next.

The silence was cracked by shouts from Gabrel, like an announcement from a heavenly trumpet.

"We found her! We found mammy!" Gabrel came running up the track as fast as he could, gasping for each breath he could suck in. "Me and Katie and Lucinda. We found her!"

Rafe, Tom and Wash all jumped up and took off after Gabrel, who had picked up his mother's bundle wrapped in her handkerchief and then tossed it to Rafe as they ran toward the pine field.

Down the path and past the thicket, Rafe stopped up short at the horrible sight of his mother. He had feared the worst, and now he was abruptly confronted by the sight of his mother lying dead on the ground. She was not alone. The buzzards had found the body a day or two earlier. Rafe ran up quickly to chase the large black birds away. They only reluctantly hopped off and flew up onto the branches of the nearby trees to observe the human intruders. Not so agreeable about leaving were the flies, which continued to buzz about and cling to the body. The stench was becoming nauseating.

Rafe had had a sense all along that the search for his mother would not end well. Nellie's body, naked from the waist up, was lying face down, with the arms and legs extended. The large hole in her back was encrusted in dried blood. Her skull bone was exposed in the large rip in the flesh that resulted from the crush of the rock. Her hair was matted in dried blood. Much of the body had been picked apart by the buzzards. Two bloody rocks lay nearby. Her head rested near a pine tree amid bright green pine seedlings shooting up all around.

The pine field was actually a rather serene place, one where workers could find respite from the toiling in the fields. The tall green and brown grass field was perfect for a picnic or quiet gathering, maybe even a praise meeting. The pine and hardwoods offered shade and protection from the gusty winds that sometimes blew through. This was not where you would expect to find such a gruesome sight. The pine field was known as a place for life, not death.

For Gabrel and the girls, their emotions were too intense to hold in. Sobbing, they turned away from the remains of their mother and consoled each other. Their moaning and wailing cut through the silence of the morning. Rafe and the others embraced them for comfort. All the Bible verses and spirituals they had ever heard growing up could never prepare these young ones for this moment. A wicked hand had moved across the land and struck their mother down. Even more fearful was the possibility that their mother had been conjured, possessed of an evil spirit. Such talk was not taken lightly in the plantation culture.

"I told mammy not ta mess with da devil," Rafe said, "cause da devil don't care nottin' for her. Da devil care only fer hisself." Rafe and Gabrel gathered up pine branches as cover for the body to keep the buzzards and flies from getting to it.

The big brother cautioned his siblings not to tell anyone of their discovery. He said he would take care to see the proper people were told about their find and that their mother's remains were collected. He left immediately to find Tom West; the two of them together took the railroad to Washington.

———◆———

The provost marshal's office was in the two-story red-brick county courthouse in the center of the Washington. Tom and Rafe presented themselves to Capt. Alfred Cooley, the military man in charge. Dapper in his crisp blue uniform and sporting a goatee, Cooley delivered the image of a military officer who was in total control of events around him. He had shown as much in battle.

The young Cooley's demeanor and military bearing were quite in contrast to the other officer who had joined them—the newly arrived sub-commissioner for the Freedmen's Bureau, Brig. Gen. Edward Wild. With one arm missing and a mangled hand, Wild did not fit the visual mold of military precision.

Tom, Rafe, the captain and the general all huddled in a small office the provost marshal otherwise used to take loyalty oaths. The black painted tables and chairs were in disarray. Stacks of papers predominated in every corner of the room. But all was shoved aside to make room for Rafe, who had a story to tell that would shatter any sense of peace on this Lord's Day.

"Rafe, I'm going to have to put you under oath to take your statement," Cooley announced. "You know what that means? That you will tell only the truth about what you know?"

"Yes, suh, I do." Rafe replied, as he sat erect in one of the chairs, eyes fixed on the floor.

"Your mother has been missing how long?" Cooley asked.

"Four days, suh. We found her body just now." Rafe replied.

"She was dead, you say?"

"Yes, Suh. Appear ta be fer some time." His voice began to tremble a bit. "Da buzzards, da had all da flesh eat offen her arms down ta her hands. Da skin had commenced ta peel off. I sees da back part of her head an' neck."

Wild looked at Cooley. He could hardly contain his anger. Wild had no love for those who used and abused negroes.

Cooley continued. "And you knew this to be your mother?"

Rafe raised his head slightly but avoided eye contact. "I knows her ta be me momma from da mole on her back...on her shoulder. An' da big toe on da right foot was cut, had a rag tied to it. No shoe on dat foots, but one on da well foots. I think da cut big toe was on da right foots."

"Anything else?" Cooley asked. A private sitting nearby was taking notes.

"I knows her by her clothes she had on an' by shots in her bundle. Momma cooked some bread dat morn' sometimes 'fore she left. I knowed she carried it wit' her in da bundle, an' I believes da bread found in dat bundle to be da same I seen her bake dat morning." Tears began to well up in the young man's eyes. The emotions he had held in for the past several hours were about to burst like a summer storm cloud.

"And she had been shot, you say?" Cooley pressed on.

"Shot in da back—a ball hole big 'nuff to stick a finger in." He could hardly get the words out. The tears flowed down his dark black face. "I finds da head lookin' smushed down 'n skin't all 'round." Fighting a sniffle in his nose, he ran his tan shirtsleeve across his face.

"Had there been problems between your mother and the overseer?"

A troubled expression enveloped Rafe's face. He knew a day of reckoning was coming. "Oh, I warned momma she must not talk 'bout bein' free; not scold or be saucy; someone be da cause of her death."

The interrogation continued for a time. Cooley prodded with questions; Rafe provided the answers. When he had heard enough, Cooley gathered a squad of his Colored Troops and headed out to the farm with Rafe in tow.

When they arrived, a sergeant greeted Brown by reading to him an order for his arrest. The soldier then asked where Reese lived. Reese was arrested the following day. The master and his acolyte were now together again and locked up in the Washington jail.

General Wild's presence at the inquiry was not unusual. The Freedmen's Bureau was tasked with resolving complaints and crimes involving negroes, sometimes operating in conflict with military authorities charged with enforcing martial law. A complaint about coloreds being mistreated or even murdered was too much for this Massachusetts native and Harvard-trained homeopathic physician to ignore, and he had caught the first train from Augusta to be in the center of events.

The ardent abolitionist joined the Freedmen's Bureau after service in the Union Army, where he lost his left arm at the Battle of South Mountain in September 1862. A year later he would be leading an expedition of U.S. Colored Troops known as "Wild's African Brigade" in a reign of terror along the North Carolina coast, freeing and recruiting slaves along the way. Wild found a great deal of joy allowing them to whip their former masters.

He made it his personal mission to redress the wrongs which had been forced on the negroes and to square up for the cruelties they had suffered under slavery. Many said he went to work to educate and elevate coloreds in complete disregard of the feelings and rights of white people.

Frustrated by the lack of respect and support he was getting from General Steedman and the Union authorities in Augusta, Wild, resplendent with a near full face of fluffy mutton chops and mustache, relished the opportunity to be involved in a murder investigation involving a negro victim.

Wild arrived in Washington in the company of another bureau representative, Rev. Mansfield French. During the war, the Methodist missionary from New York actively worked on the resettlement of fugitive slaves on South Carolina's Sea Islands. He occasionally got involved in the fighting, like the time he formed a "Gospel Army" of hymn-singing negro crusaders who burned Darien, Georgia, in July 1863.

With the end of the fighting and of slavery, which he once described as "the great antagonistic foe," French traveled across Georgia and South Carolina preaching to freedmen and planters by the tens of thousands about their obligations under emancipation.

Now, he was in Washington where the negroes eagerly accepted his teachings and his offers to conduct marriage ceremonies in Christian services. Whites were not so enthusiastic. In one of his sessions, he told the negroes that one day some of them would be called upon to rule the land—a clear reference to the unpopular idea of negro suffrage. That prompted one white to describe him as a "miserable, crack-brained fanatic."

One of Reverend French's first meetings was in Barnett's Grove, the farm of attorney Samuel Barnett, whose place was popular for community gatherings. Thousands of negroes came by the wagonload to hear about their freedom. Another of his meetings was at the mansion of fugitive secessionist Robert Toombs, who had railed on the Senate floor that one day, he would call the roll of his slaves in the shadow of the Bunker Hill monument. In a turn of justice, Reverend French, wearing his long green tailcoat and holding his beaver hat, posited himself at the door of the Toombs home, the sun reflecting off the bald spot on the top of his head. To the large crowd of negroes and whites gathered on the grounds before him, French called the roll of Toombs' slaves and concluded by reading the Emancipation Proclamation.

The preacher the blacks referred to as "White Jesus" and the terrorist general had arrived in Washington, Georgia, at a fortuitous moment.

Nellie's body had been removed to Washington for examination by the Union authorities. When it was returned to the farm, the family, as was the custom, sat up all night with it in Nellie's cabin. After the body was bathed and dressed—very difficult to accomplish considering the poor condition of Nellie's body—it rested on a white sheet draped over an ironing board. Someone offered up a wooden box they had made as a casket. Such boxes were painted whatever color could be found, usually black, as was the case with this one.

The next day family and friends gathered for a few brief words. Then they formed in procession behind the wagon carrying the box and walked to the slave cemetery out near the oat field. The sounds of moaning and hymns of mournful praise echoed across the farm as Nellie was put to her final rest.

As was the custom, the funeral would be preached a year after burial.

CHAPTER 6

———————

Crawfordville, Georgia
March 23, 1883

"Josiah, this is one fascinating tale you are sharing," I said, pushing myself to and fro in the large white rocking chair. I had become quite accustomed to the rockers on the veranda, which stretched the length of the entire front of the house.

"We're actually just getting started, Mister Wood," he responded. "You shall see that the seeds about to be planted by old General Wild will reap a bitter harvest."

"General Wild? In what way?" I was getting curious about the one-armed general.

"Let's go back to the beginning," he replied.

"Just how far back?" I wondered.

"After the war, freed people saw the Army as their protectors. That's why Nellie sought them out." Josiah began. "When the Southern Army collapsed, freedmen moved from the fields to wherever they could find the safety only men in a blue uniform could provide. And that's mostly in the cities and towns where they were garrisoned. That didn't work well for the army because it was not equipped to house, feed and otherwise take care of the surge of negroes. So the army urged the negroes to return to the farms and work out labor arrangements with the former owners."

Josiah reached down to that familiar spot under the small wooden table next to his rocker where he kept his bottle of homebrew. It was time for a sip or two. Thought to myself I better offer my glass and join him now.

"I remember some of our newspaper coverage from that time," I remarked. "The freedmen started with literally nothing, other than a debt to the white person who helped them get started in the new life." Negroes could escape the bondage of ownership but could not escape being obligated to white people, I thought to myself.

I continued, "Probably most important was that negroes finally had access to an education, to schools where they could learn to read and write. An education would seem to do more to lift them from bondage than an Emancipation Proclamation."

"In the midst of all this," Josiah said, "the Union soldiers maintained a war footing for fear of guerilla fighting and fear that moves might be made to salvage slavery. There was much lawlessness, especially where the soldiers were absent. There were also lots of rumors going around that in December, the negroes were going to arm themselves to rise up to kill the whites."

"And in Washington the irony is the peace among whites was kept by negro soldiers?" I half-stated, half-asked.

"The 156th New York Volunteer Regiment, Infantry, they were. Oh," he leaned back in his rocker, "they had quite the reputation for their wartime exploits. Louisiana, Sheridan's Shenandoah Valley campaign, the final push through North Carolina. The Mountain Legion, they were called."

For some reason I felt a history lesson was about to unfold.

"Another sip," I asked, extending my empty glass.

"Don't mind if I do," Josiah replied, filling his glass and ignoring mine.

"They came from upstate New York. Now what does a Yankee from near Canada know about the South?" Josiah asked. "Nothing!" he shouted, answering his own question.

"Many of these Northern troops looked down on the freedmen with disdain. They amused themselves playing pranks on the coloreds or had them entertaining the troops. Even working for the soldiers."

Josiah continued with his history lesson. "One of the reasons their ranks began to swell with negroes is because the Union wanted to use them for garrison duty in the South. The white soldiers had won the victory, so 'send them home,' they said. Send the coloreds to the South to keep order. Besides," Josiah added, mopping his brow with a blue polka dot handkerchief he pulled from his shirt pocket, "they take the Southern heat much better than the Yankee boys.

"So, when the white cavalry from Iowa packed out of Washington, the Colored Troops from New York came in. Tolerable bunch, I will add. Captain Cooley kept them in good order. But the presence of General Wild was alarming, even to the Union officer. Cooley said Wild and French had given him more trouble than all the Rebels he ever had to deal with.

"Wild's reputation preceded him. In the closing months of the war, newspaper articles reaching these parts were describing horrible atrocities he was responsible for—he and his boss, Major General Butler.

"One article was headlined 'A Wild General!' Wild and his negro companies were terrorizing the civilian population in North Carolina. Confiscating farms, taking civilians hostage, turning the slaves loose on the countryside. Wild found that only a more rigorous style of warfare, including burning of homes and barns, would bring subjugation. The man shows no honor," said Josiah, shaking his head.

Wild's style of warfare reminded me of General Sherman's use of "total war" in Georgia on his march to the sea. How hard Sherman must have been on the local population seemed mild compared to what Josiah was sharing about Wild.

"In one of his most brazen acts, Wild and his thirteen hundred colored troopers assembled to watch the impromptu hanging of a Confederate soldier, who Wild was convinced was actually a guerilla. The hastily made gallows malfunctioned, and when Wild kicked the barrel out from under the soldier, his neck did not snap. He did not die instantly. No. Wild left him there dangling and strangling until the life left his body.

"And that's not all." You could see by Josiah's expressions he was taking this tale very personally. "Before Wild left the scene of this atrocity, he pinned to the man's clothing a note he had previously written. It said, 'This guerrilla hanged by order of Brigadier General Wild.' You can understand why the folks in Washington would be none too pleased when he showed up."

Josiah leaned over to me and with his right index finger slid his eyeglasses down to the tip of his nose. This gesture was the sign that something important was about to come out. At least something important to him.

"The civil governments were abolished, and the military provost marshals were in charge. Period." He poked his index finger into the air to accent the point he was making. "That meant, in the absence of civilian courts, serious crimes would be settled by military commissions—panels of military officers, Yankee military officers at that—who would take evidence and render verdicts for both negroes and whites."

I added, "Including John Brown and Christopher Reese…"

"Including Brown and Reese," he repeated. "These commissions were resented by the local populous, as you might imagine."

"I can imagine," I injected.

Josiah continued. "During the war the Supreme Court ruled that military commissions were what they called article two courts, which means the justices could not hear appeals from them under the Constitution. Wasn't until well after the war that the court rebuked the authority of the President to deny Americans trial by jury.

"And Mister Wood, imagine this," Josiah shot right back. "A court where a negro could swear witness against a white man."

I was puzzled because I had not been in a courtroom that made such a distinction.

"I see the question mark on your face, sir," he continued, this time pointing his finger at my face.

"That's the way it was in the South before the war. Negroes didn't testify against whites. But for a military commission? Yes, sir—everybody testifies! And that, sir, was not a good sign for our two killers—Reese and Brown."

Josiah stood up and walked over to the railing on the porch. He struck a pose looking down on me.

I had a feeling things were about to get dramatic when he paused momentarily. "When the negro can put his hand on a bible and swear to an oath—remember, Rafe took an oath when he gave his statement to Captain Cooley—when a negro swears to that oath and starts bringing up everything under God's glorious sun that a white man ever did to him, the Yankee soldiers will buy every word of it."

With his finger raised and wagging at me, Josiah concluded. "Mark my words," he said.

I had brought with me a clipping from the *New York Times* from that summer of 1865. What the correspondent observed in Georgia at the time seemed to support the picture being painted for me. I pulled it from my pocket to share it with my host.

The writer described relations between freedmen and former owners as varied as the produce in a vegetable stand. "On one plantation of 200 persons," the report said, "but one man resumed work: on another of 60 laborers, all were moving off toward Savannah.... Farmers and planters are living in great apprehension lest their slaves, on being made fully aware that they are free, should leave them at once, causing the ruin of crops, or consent to remain only in view of extortionate wages." The writer observed that the stalemate would not be helpful for either colored or whites because getting the current crop in "is life for this people during the coming months."

Such was the pressure John Brown felt. The crop came first, and there was no denying that his tough management of his workers would get that crop to harvest. The ultimate question, though, was "at what price?" Perhaps at the cost of a former slave's life?

The *Times* article cited better race relations in the southwest and northwest portions of Georgia, where the "late slave population continue cheerfully and faithfully at their old accustomed work; masters take good care of them; they are mutually attached and neither party desires separation."

And the writer made clear that for many on the farm, emancipation was taken as a false start. "Many servants who had left their homes in the first flush of new-found freedom, not knowing what it meant, and thinking it meant, at least, that they were to move off and have an easy, idle time of it somewhere, have quickly learned the folly of such notions about as speedily as the same number of white people would have learned the same lesson, and have gladly returned to their old homes and to their former occupations."

For all the Freedmen's Bureau did to discourage idleness and promote work among the negroes, the reporter found a big challenge remained. "Whether some additional urgency of argument to persuade lazy people to work, coming in the shape of gentle, military compulsion or constraint, would be most requisite, is a question.

"The Southern people are a kind and sympathizing people, as a race; the hauteur of Northern moneyed aristocrats—doubt it who will—is unknown here. This is not a mean-spirited race, causelessly to oppress and maltreat the ignorant and the dependent classes."

So, even an outsider can sense hope. But then the writer never met John Brown or Christopher Reese. Josiah simply nodded in acknowledgement of what I had just shared with him. I tucked the article away, back in my pocket.

Since May 25, 1865, Alexander Hamilton Stephens, who is as revered in these parts as was Caesar in his empire, has been biding his time in a small, dark cell at Fort Warren, Massachusetts. Living the life of a common criminal was the price he was paying for having been a heartbeat away from the presidency of the failed Confederate States of America. Never mind his reluctance to promote the cause, he was still a war criminal.

One of his guards reported to a local newspaper that Stephens spent much of his time writing and had completed a voluminous history of the rebellion. He also read a lot and each morning spent time singing hymns. The guard said he sang "with a good voice and a lot of spirit." Stephens and former Postmaster General John Reagan had adjoining cells but were not allowed to share conversation. In fact, part of the condition of Stephens' imprisonment was that he was not supposed to have interaction with anyone.

There were no exchanges with other inmates when he took his daily walks in the prison yard, giving the other prisoners a feeling that he was being aloof. Not the case at all. However, one thing he would talk about when opportunity permitted was his dislike for Jeff Davis.

———◆———

Nellie West's disappearance was the talk of Raytown, Crawfordville, Washington—the entire region of northeast Georgia. It didn't take much to get the locals stirred up. Raw feelings against the Yankees, raw feelings about the new status of negroes and every other grievance known to man found its way into the boiling caldron of public opinion.

From his headquarters in Augusta, General Steedman reasoned that there was one person whose presence might calm the populace. That would be Alexander H. Stephens, who unfortunately was indisposed in federal custody at the time.

Steedman felt strongly enough about his reasoning that he shared his feelings in a personal letter to President Johnson on July 15 while the search for Nellie's body was still under way:

"I believe that the release of Mister Stephens—even on parole, if you can consistently do it—would gladden the heart of almost every man, woman and child in Georgia. The people—the masses—are very strongly attached to him."

Two weeks later by special order of President Johnson, Stephens would be moved to more comfortable quarters at Fort Warren, released from confinement in his cell, allowed to have the run of the fort and see visitors for the first time in his confinement. But even in such circumstances, Stephens would be of no help to calm emotions back home.

———•———

CHAPTER 7

Washington, Georgia
July 20, 1865

TALK WAS CHEAP IN THE Washington jail where Brown and Reese were being held. General Wild took over the investigation from Captain Cooley—even to the extent of putting his medical skills to use by examining the mutilated body of Nellie West. He was anxious to get a conversation going with the prisoners.

Back in the room in the courthouse where they had earlier taken Rafe's statement, Wild prepared to question a ragged-looking John Brown, who saw to it that his newly-hired legal counsel, Garnett Andrews, was present.

Brown, still wearing the blue coveralls he had on at the time of his arrest, was seated at the small black wooden table. His legs were shackled in rusty iron clamps, and his hands, cuffed at the wrist in front of him, were resting on the table.

Wild launched right into the matter at hand, asking Brown what had happened. Brown was eager to give an account.

"C. Columbus Reese killed Nellie West between 7 and 8 o'clock a.m., Thursday, July 13, 1865, near the railroad," Brown replied deliberately, nodding his head in the process.

"And why did he do this?" Wild pressed on.

"Go ahead, John," Andrews urged. "We want to get the facts out." And Brown was eager to cooperate.

"He did it because she said she was going to the Yankees, saying that the murder would never be suspicioned on him." Brown kept cutting his eyes toward his attorney as he spoke. "He said he intended to kill everyone who told him they were going to the Yankees. That he had already killed two, and that he would kill everyone who would go to the Yankees. I heard these remarks." Brown raised his hands to pump his thumbs into his chest. "They were made to me. No one else was present."

"Tell me about the shooting of the negro woman," said Wild. He was standing directly in front of Brown, with eyes locked on the prisoner.

The tale was unfolding in front of an array of witnesses, who were crowded into the small room. In addition to Wild and Andrews, present were Reese's attorney, Samuel Barnett; Provost Marshal Cooley; Freedmen's Bureau Agent French; and a hospital steward, Orlando Van Deusen. All listened intently.

Brown continued. "I was near the act when it was committed. I was near the railroad crossing, and Columbus Reese was crouching behind the bushes. I heard him pop a cap, and I heard Nellie say, 'Yes, I see you are trying to shoot at me.' I saw her run along the tracks and into a pine thicket."

Brown paused for a moment to catch his breath. His words were racing from his lips so fast they were tripping over each other.

"Reese then appeared to be putting another cap on his gun, at the same time hastening after her. I hallooed to him: 'Quit. Don't do that.' But he made no reply and ran after her into the pine. Then I heard the gun fire, and then I saw him turn around and stop.

"Nellie screamed two or three times." Brown tapped his index finger on the table to emphasize the count. "Reese came back out of the pines and asked me to shoot my double-barreled gun into her head to make sure she was dead."

"So did you?" Wild asked, leaning forward toward the table.

Shaking his head, Brown replied, "I told him I would not do it for all the money in the world. He then went back into the pines. Took a rock and threw it at her head, saying, 'If you don't shoot her with the gun, I will finish her with a rock.' He then told the reason why he did not stop when I hallooed at him after popping the cap—because she would go over to the Yankees and report that he had tried to shoot her, and that would be equally as bad as if he had done it."

It was easy to see that Brown was becoming unnerved by the questioning. While he had started with careful descriptions, he was not being so cautious now. Andrews looked on but made no effort to control his client's words.

"I did not see the bundle after we shot. Uh. After *he* shot." Brown caught himself and was quick to correct his error. Or was it an error? It was enough of a slip for him to look over to his attorney for a reassuring response. Then he continued with his story.

"I turned my back to the body and cried, so I did not see what more he did to the body. I heard him say 'Damn you, I reckon you are dead now.' Then I said, 'I would not have had this happen for all the money in the world.' And he replied that he, too, was sorry he had done it but added that 'none of them should come before him and say they are going to the Yankees without serving them the same way.'

"I cried because the deed was done and because she had been a faithful old nigger—though crippled some—and I just could not bear to think that a good old nigger should be served so for just nothing at all."

Brown might have cried a river at the scene of Nelly's death, but no tears or even red eyes were evident today as he rambled through his story.

"Then what did you do?" Wild asked.

"We turned and headed for home. We came up behind the negro quarters and passed between them into the yard, arriving at the house the same moment William—Christopher's daddy—arrived. Friday morning, C. C. left my house to return home with the gun he had used to shoot Nellie with."

"Can you describe the gun for me?"

"The gun was peculiar—rather short and scarcely any stock, only about a foot of wood in the breech, originally rifled. I never saw the balls that he fired with it. He said he bought it from Benjamin Sturtevant. I think he borrowed it, from his expression to Mister Sturtevant: 'Do you really want your gun?' I have not seen it since."

With his cohort now the topic of discussion, Brown wanted to make sure the deed did not turn back on him. He relayed a brief jailhouse conversation between the two. "Reese was very inquisitive last night to know if, in searching, the soldier has found any rifle. He wished me to say there was no rifle about the premises, even."

Wild had heard enough for now but wanted to make sure he had missed nothing important. "Is there anything else?"

Brown sat up straight in his chair. He looked over at his lawyer then locked eyes with Wild. "I did not give information about the matter earlier because my life was threatened by Columbus Reese, who told me if I ever cheeked it, he would kill me if it cost him his life to attempt it."

And Brown wasn't finished. "He threatened me thus repeatedly before the arrest and since. I feared his threats because he had told me he had killed two niggers and had shot one of his fellow soldiers in the army because he had called him a damned liar."

———

Two days after interviewing Brown, General Wild stopped by the Washington jail to question one of the guards. Rumors were flying, and Wild had latched onto a good one.

He was seated at the small table in the interview room when the door opened and a soldier walked in smartly, stopping at attention. "Thank you for meeting with me," Wild told the soldier, who stood erect before him in his blue Union uniform. "You are the one who had the conversation earlier today with prisoner Reese?"

"Yes, sir. That is correct," the soldier nervously replied, breaking his stance enough to wipe the sweat from his brow with the back of his hand. "Sir, my name is William Schribner. I was the guard on duty."

Private Schribner was but 15 years old when he joined the Union Army in Kingston, New York. Three years of chasing Rebels across the

South and dodging their deadly gunfire came to a climax on a hot summer day with an otherwise uneventful shift of guard duty at the jail in Washington, Georgia.

"Tell me what happened, private," Wild said in a manner to try to calm the lad.

"Well, prisoner Reese came to the middle door of the jail to talk with prisoner Brown through the hallway. At that point I asked Reese whether he was guilty of killing that woman, Nellie, or not."

"And how did he respond to you?" Wild inquired.

"Sir," Schribner replied, "he said he was guilty, that he shot her himself—the first one he ever shot." Schribner's eyes shifted around the room, as if searching for something to lock onto.

"Go on, son," Wild urged.

"That Brown had no hand in the killing."

Wild paused the questioning for a moment. He appreciated what he was hearing. Perhaps the statement from Brown a couple of days earlier had more than a kernel of truth to it.

The young soldier picked up the conversation. "Something was said between Brown and Reese about a rock being used. I did not hear what."

"Did Brown respond?"

"Brown heard all that Reese said to me. Brown made no reply to him, but said to me: 'You heard what he said.'"

"And you said...."

Schribner did not hesitate: "I first advised Reese to confess it, if he was really guilty, as I thought the law might lie easier upon him if he confessed it."

Again, the conversation took a pause as Wild sought to absorb what he had just learned about the prisoners. It must be correct, he reasoned. Why would the guard fabricate such a jailhouse conversation?

The general had heard enough. "Thank you, soldier. Good work."

Later in the day, Wild was joined in the interview room in the court-house by Reese; his father, William—some folks knew him as Jasper; his attorney, Sam Barnett; and a few others.

"You know why I'm here, so let's get on with this," Wild said as he took a seat at the table opposite Reese. Reese's feet were manacled and his hands cuffed in the same manner as Brown's had been during his interview.

"Yes, sir. I committed the act of killing Nellie West," Reese responded.

"Tell me what happened." Wild sat back in his chair to listen.

Reese took a deep breath. He looked over at his father, whose head was bowed, his hands covering his face. "Thursday morning, July 13, Mister Brown got me to write a note for her to take to the Yankees. I wrote it. When Missus Brown give me the paper I used, I asked Nellie where it was to go to. Nellie did not say, so I rose up." Reese started to stand, but thought better of it and sat down. "And told her I would knock her down if she did not tell me where she was going to. Ten minutes after Nellie left, Mister Brown and I went on a walk together with guns."

"Go on," Wild urged. Reese's father's eyes were now focused on his son. As forlorn as Christopher Reese looked in the soiled pants and shirt he had been wearing since his arrest, his voice was firm and clear.

"We were on the road near the railroad tracks where we saw her. She caught sight of me, and I crouched down. She said to Mister Brown that she saw me trying to shoot her. Brown told me with a wink what Nellie had just said."

This time Reese looked over at Barnett, who urged him to continue with the story.

"Brown first proposed to kill Nellie soon after leaving the house, saying it would never do to let her get to Washington, as she would get us into a scrape if we did not kill her. And that I would get into a scrape just as much as he would."

"So you shot her?" Wild asked.

"We walked after Nellie along the track. She said she was going to the depot to take the train. We walked about two hundred yards along the railroad, then turned into the woods. She hurried, and Brown called to her to stop. Then she dropped her bundle and began to run, stumbling under the limbs."

Reese picked up the pace of the narrative and in a raised voice proclaimed, "Brown called out to me: 'Shoot! Shoot! Shoot!'"

Reese paused. His head dropped to the table and tears began falling from his swelling, reddened eyes. As he continued the narrative, his voice got softer. William, his father, turned away.

"I fired at her at about thirty yards. She ran five or ten paces and fell and hallooed three or four times. Brown was about five paces behind me, and I told him to fire. He said nothing, but ran up to where she was. I again asked him to shoot. He looked at her and said it was not any use. He picked up a stone and told me to throw it at her, and I threw the stone and hit her on the head. 'She ain't dead yet,' Brown said, so he handed me a bigger stone to throw at her which hit her shoulder."

Wild sat calmly, taking in the prisoner's story line-by-line, very matter-of-factly. "How did Brown react?"

"Mister Brown did not cry. He laughed there, and laughed all the way home, and patted me on the shoulder and praised me up. He laughed at home during the day, slyly at me." Reese raised his head from the table and looked straight at his father.

"I told him never to tell of the killing, as I had done it only to accommodate him. He said he would never tell. He would spend the last drop of his blood first."

"Is there anything else, son?" asked Wild.

"Nothing was ever said about burying her."

With that, Reese got up from his chair. His father walked over to him and hugged him, the guards stepping aside to accommodate them. They exchanged unintelligible whispers, amid sobs and tears. When their grip was released, Christopher was escorted from the room and returned by the guards to the jail.

Two witnesses, in fact the *only* witnesses, had given their testimony in two different and contradictory versions. Just who to believe? The answer to that question would have to wait because General Wild seemingly had discovered more pressing business.

In this summer after the war, the countryside was awash in lawlessness, as could be expected with the breakdown of civil authority. Union troops were often the targets of bushwhackers, who would lay in wait and shoot at passing soldiers. Other former Confederates would infiltrate camps at night to slit the throats of soldiers. Union sympathizers and freedmen were the objects of untold deprivations.

It was in this environment that General Wild picked up some talk about the robbery in late May of a train of five wagons returning several hundred thousand dollars of gold and silver from Washington to Richmond. The Virginia bankers secured an order for the safe passage of their bank reserves, which had been in a bank vault in Washington for safekeeping since the fall of Richmond to the Yankees back in April.

So as not to arouse undue attention, the wagons had simple white canvas coverings and offered no clues as to the treasure of coins and bars of precious metals contained inside each. General Upton provided a small army escort for the journey, which would take the train of wagons to Lisbon to cross the Savannah River. But, no doubt, someone was tipped off. After the party had bedded down for the night near the 400-acre Chenault Plantation, about 12 miles out of Washington, robbers struck the camp with great surprise.

Resistance was useless. There was much calamity and confusion as the raiders plundered the wagons and filled their pockets and sacks with all they could gather. The men were said to have waded ankle deep in shiny gold and silver bars and coins. Their horses were so weighted down that many had to throw away some of what they had collected in order to make their getaway. As quickly as the raid began, it was ended without a shot fired—or a throat slit.

When word of the robbery reached Washington, Gen. E. Porter Alexander collected a company of former members of the home guard to recover the treasure, and, if possible, detain the perpetrators. They did locate a good portion of what was taken, but an equally large amount had vanished into the night.

Even though the robbery had occurred almost two months earlier and the trail had become as cold as a New York winter, Wild could not resist the challenge—or temptation—to find the missing treasure. He gathered a dozen of Captain Cooley's Colored Troops and made haste to the scene of the crime, where he was met by the plantation owner, a prominent Methodist minister and unreconstructed secessionist, Dionysus Chenault. Prior to emancipation, Chenault was also one of the largest slave owners in Lincoln County with a count of nearly two dozen.

"Nish," as he was called, and his family denied any involvement in the robbery. Nonetheless, Wild ordered the men strung up by their thumbs—quite a strain for the 300-pound preacher—and the women strip searched. When his torture failed to bring forth any admissions, Wild took the women to the courthouse in Washington, where he locked them up in a jury room and put them on a diet of bread and water.

Attorney John Weems, who was now defending John Brown in the murder case, went with two others to confront Wild to obtain the release of the Chenault women. No reason to detain them, Weems argued: "The tortures and indignities thus inflicted upon this family, who are respected and esteemed by all who knew them, failed to discover any evidence whatever of their complicity in the robbery...." And the General's response? According to Weems, he "promptly and emphatically refused."

On behalf of the Chenault family, Brown's other attorney, Garnett Andrews, interceded directly with the Union Commander for the Department of Georgia. General Steedman was incensed at Wild's conduct. He ordered the women released and sent one of his staff members, Colonel Drayton, to Washington to investigate Wild's activities there personally. Wild had also incurred much wrath among the local population when he seized the home of Confederate leader Robert Toombs and put Toombs' wife out on the street.

In a letter on August 15 to President Johnson, Steedman referenced his problems with the agents from the Freedmen's Bureau, describing Wild as "weak" and "fanatical." He complained that Wild had caused "some trouble, and occasioned a good deal of alarm in the minds of the people.…"

German-born Maj. Gen. Carl Schurz, an emissary of President Johnson's, observed in a separate report that Wild was "totally unfit for the discharge of the duties incumbent upon him." He didn't stop there: "He displays much vigor where it is not wanted, but shows little judgment where it is wanted."

Even Lt. Col. Joseph S. Fullerton, the Adjutant General for the Freedmen's Bureau, observed, "I really believe that he is a little crazy."

As a result of Drayton's inquiry, on September 12, Wild was formally relieved of his duties with the Freedmen's Bureau in Georgia. He was unceremoniously sent to Washington, D.C., where charges were preferred against him. Weems would later share his frustration over the lack of further information about any discipline, saying that "the public is not advised that even as much as a reprimand was ever administered to him."

Wild was never seen again in Washington, Georgia, but that didn't mean he would never be heard from again. His shadow would loom large over the military commission's upcoming proceedings.

Several days after hearing Reese's confession, Wild reached a conclusion. Not content to be the investigator, he offered his own judgment. He believed that the truth actually was being told by John Brown because Brown said he had no part in the murder and Reese's statements to the guard backed him up. Wild volunteered for the record a written statement that supported Brown's versions of events:

In the case of John M. Brown and Christopher Columbus Reese, accused of murdering Nellie West, I was occupied in collecting evidence for the prosecution, and when said Brown showed a disposition to tell what he knew, I promised a recommendation to the mercy of the court in consideration of his turning state's evidence in this case.

Wild's statement may have given Brown pause to believe his nightmare would soon end. But he would later find the words from the general were far from comforting.

—————◆—————

Within a few days of their questioning by Wild, the prisoners were scheduled to be relocated to the jail in Augusta for their own safety. In Augusta they would be far from the trouble that was brewing in the streets of Crawfordville and Washington, and far from their families— and attorneys.

But before the transfer from the Washington jail, Reese would have one last visitor—Caroline Garrett. Yes, that Caroline, the stepdaughter of John Brown. The woman whose affections Reese had sought. The prize Brown promised to give him—along with five dollars—for killing Nellie West.

Reese, of course, was pleased to see her. "Caroline, thank you so much for coming."

Caroline observed her pitiful friend through the iron bars of the cell. As sweet and soft and perfect as her features looked to her would-be suitor, Reese was disheveled and unkempt. His hair was shaggy and his beard scraggly. His frame thin. His face gaunt. It was not the look Caroline would expect of a gentleman who would want to come calling.

"Lum, I just don't know how you and Pa could have gotten yourselves in such a stew," she replied. The reference to Brown, her stepfather, as her "Pa" clearly showed whose side she had taken. Family, after all, was much more important that would-be suitors.

Caroline made sure Reese knew that things were far from well at home for him: "And your father is taking this really bad."

"Hush," said Reese, putting his finger to his lips and moving closer to the bars. "Neither of us will be killed."

"Why?" Caroline asked with a look of puzzlement. What an absurd statement, she must have thought. Surely someone would be held accountable for killing the woman.

"Because I killed a negro," Reese said without emotion. The young man obviously was under the illusion of pre-Reconstruction justice. Yes, before the war, a jury more than likely would have let him walk because of who the victim was. But these were different times.

Caroline was more concerned about what would happen to her stepfather. "Did Pa help you?"

"No, I done it by myself." This was not the first time Reese had minimized Brown's involvement. Was he saying this because it was true, or was he saying this to please his beautiful visitor?

Reese explained to Caroline that he had expected to keep the events of that July day a secret unto himself, but her father's earlier statement to the general forced him to come forward.

"I never would have told," he assured her, "if he had not told on me!"

CHAPTER 8

Liberty Hall
Crawfordville, Georgia
March 23, 1883

I HAD ENJOYED THE CONVERSATIONS with Josiah, Stephens' nephew and former law clerk. He was a wealth of information—and had quite a remarkable memory. But it didn't hurt that he had access to Stephens' extensive legal, political and personal files.

"I stopped to visit Mister Stephens' gravesite on the way over this morning," I said as I once again climbed those steps to the porch of Liberty Hall.

"You know, it's amazing how many of those yellow, red, blue and orange flowers still show a bit of life, what with the funeral about two weeks ago," Josiah replied.

"Hope I'm not imposing on you," I commented, as he led me through the house and into a back room that served as Alec Stephens' library and office. The walls were lined with shelves holding hundreds of volumes. A couple of leather chairs, a sofa, small tables and a desk filled out the room.

"This," Josiah started, "was Uncle's favorite room. He spent hours a day writing, reading and entertaining visitors in here. This room is actually part of the original house that was on the property. He had the old house torn down and the new house built up around these couple of rooms."

"I hope I'm not overstaying my welcome, Josiah."

"Oh, not one bit, Mister Wood," he responded.

"I mean I've lingered here much longer than I anticipated."

"Mister Wood, you best plan to keep that hotel room for a while. We're just getting started," Josiah said with a broad smile.

I couldn't imagine what was ahead. A simple trial? It seemed like an easy enough case to settle with plenty of guilt for both Brown and Reese to share. Or was it really going to be that simple? And what about Alexander Stephens? No mention of his involvement up to this point. After all, that's what I came to find out.

"I think you must remember what conditions were like that summer in Georgia." Josiah would know, because he had lived it. "Just a couple weeks after the murder, Capt. A. P. Ketchum, the Freedmen's Bureau representative in Savannah, wrote to his superior: 'The rebel spirit is as bitter as ever in the minds of the Southern people.' And General Schurz observed: 'Conflicts between whites and blacks are not unfrequent, and in many instances, result in bloodshed.'

"A boiling pot is a good way to describe it, as we've discussed previously, Mister Wood." Josiah paused. "I cannot overstate that, and I think this letter from Eliza Andrews will make that clear. I found it in Uncle's files."

"Eliza Andrews? Haven't heard that name before." I was puzzled.

"She's Garnett Andrews' daughter—you know, Brown's lawyer."

"Who also helped the Chenault family with their troubles, I recall you said."

"She fancies herself as a writer, and she shared some of her thoughts on this case with Uncle Alec. She sent a letter to him at Fort Warren, she did. Likely it was written not long after the murder happened."

Josiah picked up a piece of yellowed paper from a side table. I found it hard to make out the writings, but he had no problem reading it to me:

That murder case into which General Wild and Dr. French have been prying for the last week has wrought these apostles up to a state of boundless indignation, and father is afraid it will bring their vengeance upon the town.

"Did I tell you that she didn't care much for Yankees?" Josiah asked. "But I guess you could figure that for yourself."

He read more from the note:

I don't think he feels any too much respect for his clients, though it is his duty to make out the best case he can for them. He don't say much about the case because conversation on such subjects nearly always brings on a political row in the family, and we are all so afraid of starting a fracas that we are constrained and uneasy whenever anything touching on politics, no matter how remotely, is mentioned.

Josiah looked up from the note at me and said in a soft tone, "Wouldn't you like to be a guest at that dinner table? Wow!"

His eyes dropped back to the paper.

From the little I have heard father tell, I am afraid the murder is a very ugly affair. It seems his clients are accused of having killed an old negro woman because she left her master's plantation to go off and try the blessings of freedom. She certainly was an old fool, but I have never heard yet that folly was a capital offense.

I could see that Josiah was enjoying the message from that continuous smile on his face. He went on reading, adjusting his eyeglasses a bit.

In spite of the stench, father says General Wild examined the body with ghoulish curiosity, even pulling out the broken ribs and staring at them. All the while the old woman's son stood looking on with stolid indifference, less moved than I would be over the carcass of a dead animal. General Wild was bred a doctor and didn't seem to mind the most sickening details.

Father says he would rather have the sharpest lawyer in Georgia as his opposing counsel than these shrewd, painstaking Yankees. Captain Cooley was sent out to collect evidence, and even brought back the stone which was said to be the one with which the poor old creature was beaten on the head.

Josiah turned to me and lowered the note into his lap. "Mister Wood, Eliza was clearly an outspoken young lady. With very strong opinions, too. And very protective of her father, even though they were on different sides of secession."

I nodded in agreement, and Josiah resumed reading:

There is only negro evidence for all these horrors, and nobody can tell how much of it is false, but that makes no difference to the Yankee court. Father thinks one of the men is sure to hang, and he has very little hope of saving the other. The latter is a man of family, and his poor wife is at Mrs. Fitzpatrick's hotel almost starving herself to death from grief. She has left her little children at home by themselves, and she says when the Yankees were there to arrest their father, they were so frightened that two of them went into convulsions; they had heard such dreadful things about what the Yankees had done during the war.

The younger of the two accused men is only twenty years old, and his poor old father hangs around the courtroom, putting his head in every time the door is opened, trying to catch something of what is going on. He is less privileged than our dog Toby, who follows father to the courthouse every day and walks about the room as if it belongs to him, smelling the Yankees, and pricking up his ears as if to ask what business they had there.

Father says he would not, for millions, have had such a case as this one under the eyes of the Yankees just at this time, for they will believe everything the negroes say and put the very worst construction on it. Brutal crimes happen in all countries now and then, especially in times of disorder and upheaval such as the South is undergoing, but the North, fed on Mrs. Stowe's lurid pictures, likes to believe such things are habitual among us, and this horrible occurrence will confirm them in their opinion.

"That's quite a tome," I commented as Josiah placed the paper back onto the table and refilled his water glass. "Eliza—you say her name is?—Miss Andrews is quite an opinionated young lady."

"The Andrews are quite the family indeed. Garnett and his wife Annulet had eight children, including that fiercely Southern patriot daughter and a son who went off to war with the Confederate Army. Yet the father's heart was literally broken by secession.

"Garnett Andrews—actually James Garnett Andrews; he dropped the James—studied law under Col. Duncan G. Campbell. Campbell's son John became an Associate Justice on the U.S. Supreme Court."

"I hear he was a good lawyer, well respected."

"Oh, yes," responded Josiah. "And a master storyteller." I nodded in response. "He always found something entertaining in the courtroom. I remember one story in particular," said Stephens as he tilted his head back slightly and rubbed the greying scruff on his chin.

"They brought a very devout Methodist minister into court to discredit the testimony of one of his neighbors. And when the question was put to him, he responded, 'I do not know anything in the world against my neighbor, except that he is a Baptist. But for that, I would believe him as soon as any man in the world.'"

We both let out a hardy laugh. I could only imagine sitting with such a learned jurist and hearing such tales directly from him.

"What about a political past?" I inquired. "Did he have one?"

"Andrews spent about eighteen years on the bench, before jumping into politics. In 1855, the No Nothings put Andrews on their ticket in the election for Governor, which he lost. Five years later he bucked public opinion by opposing secession, and, you know, voters must have admired his wisdom and integrity because they gave him a seat in the legislature anyway. His love of the Union led him to vote against the secession ordinance.

"He continued his practice of the law in Washington during the war. When it was over, he thought his loyalty to the Union would lead to better things for him personally. But this case really vexed him."

"He wasn't Brown's only attorney?" I asked, now taking my own notes.

"He was assisted by John Weems, who had tried to get General Wild to release the Chenault women from his captivity. Weems was highly regarded too, having served as a colonel in the Confederate Army and been wounded on the field of fire at Savage Station and Gettysburg. In fact, he had been made the post commandant over in Washington just before the Yankees arrived. Yes, Brown had a powerful legal team, but as Eliza pointed out, they had an uphill fight on their hands."

"And what about Reese? Who represented him?" I asked.

"Samuel Barnett. He is as slick as they come. You'll see." There was that smile across Josiah's face again. "He graduated top of his class in Columbia at South Carolina College and taught school here until around 1847, when Judge Andrews admitted him to practice the law. Clean shaven, short hair. He always looked so proper, as he should, being president of the bank and a director of the Georgia Railroad. They even named that station at Barnett for Sam."

"So, how did he end up in a courtroom?"

"Charming, warm and witty. That's what they say about him. He and Isaiah Irvin, speaker of the state House, set up the practice. Had a good one too, until Irvin was killed in a steamboat accident in Texas at the beginning of the war. But Sam carried on the practice. Success in court in those days was based on who you knew, not how much of the law you absorbed. Sam made it a point to know everyone.

"And I've just got to share this with you. We've all heard it so many times." Josiah wiped his shiny brow with his handkerchief. "Sho is hot." I nodded in agreement. "Anyway, in 1846, when he was still teaching, Sam married Elizabeth Stone, his fifth cousin. His health wasn't good when he married, and doctor Ficklen predicted in five or six years, Elizabeth would be a widow." I continued to nod in agreement, not knowing where this was headed. "Well, Sam went on to outlive the doctor by thirty years!"

So much for introductions to members of the bar. Josiah had other ideas. "I think it's time we served up a bit of the homebrew because this story is about to get real serious," he said invitingly. This time he reached down under the table and pulled up a now-familiar brown bottle. He poured each of us a swallow or two. I had stopped counting the number two days ago. Maybe that's why I was sleeping so well.

"The trial for Brown and Reese was set before a military commission in Special Order Number 30 issued by the Assistant Adjutant General, T.G. Seefe, at the Headquarters of the District of Augusta, Fourth Division, Department of Georgia on September 8, 1865. Here's a copy of the order," and he handed me the yellowed sheet of paper.

"So when did the trial itself actually begin?" I asked, while skimming the order.

"They had a time getting everyone together. First they met in Athens on September 11, but one of the members was already detailed to another commission. It wasn't until October 5th the members of the Commission assembled at 10 o'clock in the courtroom in Washington to open the trial." Josiah handed me another sheet of paper.

I looked over the names of the soldiers detailed to sit on the panel. From the 156th New York, volunteers were the Provost Marshal Capt. Alfred Cooley, and Capts. Charles B. Western and John H. Palmer. From the 13th Connecticut Volunteers were 1st Lt. George H. Pratt and 2nd Lt. Herbert C. Baldwin. The prosecutor, called the judge advocate in military terms, was Capt. T. James Rundle of the 156th New York Volunteers.

These men were not in Washington for recreation. Their regiments had seen some fierce fighting—both were engaged in the siege of Port Hudson, the Red River Campaign and Cedar Creek, among others. With the war over, the men shared a common desire to be mustered out and head back home. Perhaps they had already overstayed their welcome. On the march to Augusta from Savannah, one veteran of the

13th Connecticut said the locals along the route "looked with little favor upon the Yankee invaders, as they termed us."

"So, everyone is gathered in the courtroom over in Washington— the commission members, prosecutor, defense lawyers and prisoners. First thing that happened was that Andrews objected to Captain Cooley hearing the case," Josiah volunteered.

"Let me guess." I had covered enough court cases when I was a cub reporter to take an educated stab at this one. "Since he was Provost Marshal, Cooley had heard evidence in the case under oath, specifically Rafe West's initial statement among others, and therefore is believed to have formed an opinion."

"Right you are!" Josiah replied. "And Captain Cooley was excused. Now the stage is set for Andrews to try to get the whole case thrown out."

"How's that?" I asked. "There's no other court to go to."

"Andrews based his objection on three legal principles." I could see Josiah was enjoying giving me a legal education. "One, the trial violates the third article of the Constitution which requires a trial by jury. Two, under the Articles of War, the military cannot try a civilian, except as a spy. And three, Brown has committed no crime against the military."

"And……." I hung on the word a moment to prod for a resolution.

Josiah jumped right in. "And the commission disagreed on each point. So with the formalities out of the way, it was time for the proceedings to begin."

I had heard the arguments before that lawyers used to try to get their cases thrown out of the military's criminal justice system. But each time they were rebuffed. The Union government was determined to use the commissions to enforce martial law as long as a state of war existed. And Congress was in no hurry to end the state of war, even though the fighting was long over.

CHAPTER 9

———◆———

Wilkes County Courthouse
Washington, Georgia
October 5, 1865

THIS WAS A DAY OF anticipation in Washington. The long-awaited murder trial was finally beginning. Prisoners were brought to the courtroom from the county jail, where they had been held after being brought back from Augusta. The white townsfolk who had been talking about this day for weeks were congregating on the courthouse grounds. Buggies of all descriptions, farm wagons and horses all ringed the gathering.

Stately oak trees that provided shade on summer days had lost their leaves in the transition to fall. The brown pine needles had begun falling from the long leaf pines, and grass, what grass there was, was turning brown. The grounds were in transition, much as were the people now gathered on it.

The courthouse grounds were as much for commerce as they were for justice. People used the gathering to sell and trade for all kinds of goods, including bacon, tobacco, flour, molasses, sugar, eggs, chickens and even cash, if any was to be had. A couple of musicians even showed up with fiddle and banjo to keep the atmosphere light.

The negroes, meanwhile, kept to themselves across the street. Their number was not as large as the white gathering because most had to be at work on this crisp fall morning. In fact, most of them were related to the West family in some fashion or another. A tall, sophisticated-looking man at one point appeared to be leading the group in an emotional prayer.

As if on cue, people began to file into the courthouse. The bench seats in the courtroom filled quickly—with white folks. The negroes climbed the steps up into the gallery to take their seats, as they had been trained to do during times of slavery.

All attention was drawn to the front of the courtroom, where a table was set up for the four military officers who would decide this case. Behind them, to the consternation of the unreconstructed spectators, hung a flag of the United States. The locals would consider such a flag to be a desecration of the courtroom. But they would just have to get over that for now.

Waiting for the commission to enter the room at separate tables were Brown and his two attorneys, Andrews and Weems, and Reese with his lawyer, Samuel Barnett. A formidable legal team had been arrayed against the lone government prosecutor at his table, Captain Rundle.

Brown and Reese looked back into the sea of people for glimpses of their families, who had properly seated themselves on benches just behind the railing which separated the spectators from the participants. Both families were well known in these parts. And well thought of, at least up until now. Friends and the curious joined to fill the room. And then there was Nellie West's family. The children, the aunts, the uncles, the cousins—so many here to get their first taste of this newfound justice. Or so they hoped. Their heads could be seen peering over the gallery railing, out of sight and out of mind of the white folks below.

In an instant the room got quiet when all were told to stand. The four military officers, walking erect in their crisp, blue uniforms, sabers rattling at their sides, filed to the table to take their seats. Each placed his hat on the table in front of him. The commission president, Captain Western, rapped the gavel and called for order.

"Order. Order." His voice echoed through the cavernous chamber. Conversations faded into an occasion whisper, and all others in the room took their seats.

Uniformed U.S. Colored Troops from the 156th New York were standing watch in strategic locations around courtroom. Aside from guarding the prisoners, they were present to maintain order in an atmosphere where emotions ran high.

The people of Washington were about to get a taste of justice, both military and Northern. Would the people embrace the new way? Could Western keep control of his courtroom? Would the outcome be accepted by the community? So many unknowns hung in the balance as the proceedings began.

In his deep baritone voice, Captain Western addressed the defendants, one by one.

"Will the accused Christopher C. Reese, please stand."

Reese slowly stood up, along with Barnett, his attorney. He nervously glanced back at his mother and father, seated behind him. The 20-year old farm boy, who rode to war with the Confederate Cavalry while still a teen and was on a first-name basis with the word "trouble," was about to be held accountable for perhaps the first time in his life. Reese stood erect with what military bearing he had retained from his service, facing the panel.

"Captain Swaine, please read the charge and specification," the president requested.

"In the case of Christopher C. Reese, the charge is Murder." Reese looked over at the officer and dropped his head. "The specification reads, 'In this: that Christopher C. Reese, a citizen of the State of Georgia and the United States, did willfully, unlawfully and maliciously shoot and kill Nellie West, a colored woman. This on or about the thirteenth of July 1865 in or near Taliaferro County, State of Georgia.'"

The West family responded from the gallery with loud moaning. Some of Reese's family sounded openly defiant, shouting "An outrage!" "He's innocent!"

Captain Western removed his eyeglasses and rapped the gavel loudly. Looking up into the gallery and across the courtroom, Western admonished the spectators: "There will be no conversation from those who are here gathered. This is an official judicial proceeding, and I must ask everyone to remain quiet and respect order. Or you will have to leave the premises."

Turning back to Reese, the commission president then asked how the defendant pleaded.

Reese said nothing. He turned to look at his lawyer, who then responded on behalf of his client, "To the specification: Guilty. To the charge: Guilty, your honor." Then the two quietly sat down. What an explosive announcement!

A collective gasp was sounded in the courtroom. Clearly no one was prepared for Reese to have admitted his role in the murder. Not even Brown and his attorneys could grasp what was about to happen. Nellie's family was especially pleased with the admission from Reese. Lots of smiles and hugs broke out among them. Even a few shouts of "Thank you, Jesus!"

Reese's family and friends sat in stunned disbelief. They clearly had not been prepared for this outcome. Has he signed a death warrant for certain? They could not know the course this trial would now take.

Captain Western lightly tapped his gavel, and folks quickly quieted down.

Brown and his attorneys were next to stand. Brown had an air of confidence about him. Maybe a bit too much for his own good. Capt. P. T. Swaine, who was the Judge Advocate for the Augusta District, then read the charge and specification in the case of John Brown. Brown took a moment to look out into the courtroom, making eye contact with his wife, Sara, and their children.

For all the pure hate and meanness that Brown had shown time and again against the most defenseless people who were now gathered in this courtroom in the name of their battered and murdered matriarch, would Brown finally be held accountable?

"In the case of John M. Brown," Captain Swaine began, "the charge is Murder. And the specification reads: 'In this: that John M. Brown, a citizen of Georgia and of the United States, after threatening the life of

Nellie West, a colored woman, by saying he would dash her brains out, or words to the same effect, did aid and abet one Christopher C. Reese in willfully, unlawfully and maliciously shooting and killing Nellie West. All this on or about the thirteenth of July, 1865, in or near Taliaferro County in the State of Georgia.'"

A stunned silence gripped the room, as all ears waited to hear how Brown would respond. If Reese pleaded guilty, might not Brown do the same in order to end this nightmare here and now?

After what seemed like an eternity, Captain Western put the question directly to Brown. "How do you plead?"

Attorney Garnett Andrews was the first to speak. His response on behalf of his client was not a plea, but a request. Puzzled looks filled the courtroom. Even the members of military commission were a bit perplexed. "Your honor, Mister Brown requests the court grant him until 3 o'clock p.m. today for the purpose of consulting with his counsel and proposing any pleas or demurrer which it may be necessary for him to make."

Again the courtroom became quite animated. Nellie's family had no collective understanding of what they had just heard. Did he do it, or didn't he? They were expecting a "no" and hoping for a "yes." But got neither.

Brown's family and supporters were shocked. What kind of legal maneuvering was under way? Where was the "not guilty" they had eagerly anticipated? As their conversations got louder, Captain Western again tapped the gavel.

The four members of the commission huddled in a circle of blue behind their table. They could be heard talking, but speaking much too softly to be understood. Then they again took their places as the table. As they settled in, the room again quieted down.

Western announced that the commission had denied Brown's request.

So for a second time, the president asked the question, "How does the defendant plead?"

This time Andrews replied, "To the specification: not guilty. To the charge: not guilty." Andrews then went on to argue: "Mister Brown demurs to the charge and specifications upon the ground that no sufficient crime is alleged that requires a plea."

"I object, Mister President," boldly shouted Captain Swaine. He was a West Point graduate and late in the war a commander of troops at the Battle at Kennesaw Mountain and the Siege of Atlanta. A career soldier, he actually had held the rank of Brevet Colonel for "faithful and meritorious services during the rebellion."

Andrews continued, turning now toward Swaine: "There is no allegation that Mister Brown unlawfully, willfully and maliciously aided Christopher Reese in the murder of Nellie West."

"Mister Chairman," Swaine began as he addressed the panel of four officers. "This is an outrage! Captain Rundle will present evidence clearly showing that Brown is up to his neck in this ugly affair, regardless of what his learned counsel might say. He was present. He directed the actions of his young apostle. He attempted to cover it up."

The time for arguing was over. The president was now looking directly at Andrews. "Mister Andrews, your client is going to stand trial. And testimony will begin in this courtroom tomorrow morning, promptly at 9 a.m."

End of discussion. There would be no legal gymnastics with Western presiding. The 24-year-old New Yorker had rapidly risen through the ranks, following his enlistment as a sergeant almost three years earlier to the day the trial began. After being tested by some of the toughest soldiers the South could put onto the field of battle, maintaining control of this commission proceeding would be like conducting a Sunday school class for him.

The gavel came down on the table, this time with a loud thud!

"We are adjourned!" Western declared.

CHAPTER 10

———————

Liberty Hall
Crawfordville, Georgia
March 24, 1883

"JUSTICE, IF YOU CAN CALL it that, was a peculiar institution around here before the war," Josiah explained.

"How's that?"

He continued, "The local judge was the law of the land. His decision was the only decision that mattered."

I replied with a puzzled look, "In what way?"

"He was the final say. There was no place to appeal a decision of the judge or even complain if you didn't like the outcome. The courts were completely independent."

"And at one time Garnett Andrews was one of these judges?" I asked.

"He sure was. His territory covered from here to way up into the foothills. The North Georgia Circuit, they called it." Josiah reached down and pulled out a book covered in brown paper from a briefcase next to his chair. "Judge Andrews wrote this book about ten years ago. Titled *Reminiscences of an Old Georgia Lawyer.* I want you to have this because it tells us a lot about Judge Andrews' thinking and his respect for the law."

"Thank you, Josiah." I extended my hand to retrieve the red book with a golden engraved cover. "That's very thoughtful of you. I'm sure this will be helpful in my understanding of someone who is so central to this affair."

"In the book he talks about when he came to the bar about sixty years ago. There was no legal digest. No set of procedural rules. No Supreme Court. Every circuit judge, he says, was supreme in the counties he served. There were no precedents for the court to fall back on. Lawyers were in the dark about how to proceed with their cases. More likely than not, Judge Andrews says, the cases were not tried on their merits.

"That's the old justice in Georgia," Josiah emphasized. "The military commissions brought us a new kind of justice, before the legislature got around to establishing a unified court system. We were not used to strict rules of procedure and evidence or legal precedents. This new environment was one in which our lawyers were strangers, an environment very unlike the way Judge Andrews conducted his own courtroom for those many years. Very different, as we heard during the arraignment before Captain Western. Totally different."

Josiah certainly had a good grasp of the legal profession, and his insight was becoming extremely important to my own understanding of the story that was unfolding before me.

We cut our conversation short because it was time for another trip to Raytown.

———◆———

I wanted to visit the West Plantation. I wanted to see where the crime had occurred. This time Josiah was eager to engage. So off we rode, tightly packed into the one seat on his buggy, headed east on the Wrightsboro Road.

"Git up," Josiah commanded the big black horse as we rode along, its mane flapping in the breeze. I was sure he called the name of the horse, but it was not something I remembered. No doubt the horse had a name because everything in the South has a name. Even the bugs that you can't see—called no-see-ums.

I remembered riding out on my own a couple days earlier, watching the magnificent sun posed atop the tall pines in the east. I thought back to how peaceful the ride had been. But this time, something started stirring in the back of my mind when we crossed the railroad tracks at Raytown Station and turned to head north along a dusty and potholed path. We were going to a murder scene.

After a bit Josiah turned the buggy back across the railroad tracks to come in on the main road to the house where the Brown family had once lived. Approaching the house, I could see the prominent piazza that stretched across the entire length of the front. The structure itself was a large one-story rectangular box covered in white clapboard with a silver tin roof. Clearly it had been a long time since the house had been cared for. The whitewash was faded. Some of the windows were broken out. Thick patches of weeds had taken over the gardens.

No one was home. Given the state of the house and property, I would have been surprised to find anyone there. Josiah told me that hard times had left the home abandoned for the past half dozen or so years. He led me up the front steps and into a wide hallway covered in faded and ripped yellow-flowered wallpaper. To the left was the doorway to a large square room containing small bed frames and a scattering of abandoned toys. This was probably the children's room. On the opposite side of the hallway were two other doors. One led to a more private room in the back that John and Sara probably shared. A single large black steel bedframe was in the center of the room, flanked by two small, faded white wooden tables.

The other door on the right led into a small room on the front of the house. In it by the window sat a small desk. Would that be where Christopher Reese wrote the note for Nellie to take to the Yankees? "I'll bet it was," Josiah volunteered. I was surprised to see odd pieces of furniture in the rooms. In some ways, it was like the people left, expecting one day to return.

Beyond the desk on the opposite side of the room was a door that led to the breakfast room where the family would eat their meals. Nellie's daughter Lucinda spent meal time keeping the flies off the table. And it's the same room where Brown sent Nellie after telling her she could not take her daughter with her to Washington.

On the far side beyond the large wooden farm table were the steps into the backyard and the well and the cook house. This is the yard where Brown choked Nellie and threatened to kill her in her last hours of her life. Where Reese threatened to hit her with a chair. Farther across the yard were the small cabins and log houses that made up the negro quarters.

Over to the side of the house was the hen house, where a blood-stained whipping pole stood out prominently. Brown would tie a victim to the pole using a long rope attached through a pulley. After tying the victim's feet, he would strip the victim naked and give a savage beating. After freedom for the slaves, Brown was less inclined to use the pole, but it endured as a constant reminder to the farm workers.

Off beyond the yard were the oat shocks, well overgrown and nearly unrecognizable today. This was the field Brown referred to when trying to convince his help that the pigs had been disruptive—as part of his plan to cover up the murder. Farther to the west was the long-abandoned wheat stubble pasture, not giving any hint of the above average harvest cut by the freedmen that summer. Sara Brown did not like the cows to use this field because the grazing made the milk taste funny.

Walking around to the front of the house, gazing across the road, Josiah pointed out to me the pen where the cows were kept and beyond it up on a rise the corn field where Nellie's family had been working that fateful morning. And off to the right of that field were the old pine pasture and the railroad tracks where Nellie would meet her demise.

"I've not been out here since the summer of the murder," Josiah confessed. "Really hasn't changed much from what I remember."

"I was surprised, Josiah, to find any furniture in the house at all, considering no one has lived here for a stretch."

"Not that unusual, Mister Wood," he replied. "We Southerners are neighborly folk and like to share our things. Not unusual to leave things behind for the next occupant. Besides, some of it might belong to the owner of the farm."

Josiah seemed to have an answer for everything...so far.

We got back into the buggy and rode the short distance to the old pine pasture. Being unattended for some time, the pine seedlings had grown quite a bit, and the mature pines were soaring toward the clouds.

I wanted to see just where Nellie had been killed, so I walked over to the railroad crossing where the shiny metal rails cut the dirt road in half. Standing in the middle of the tracks, I looked to the north. Nine miles up that line was Washington, Nellie's destination. Four miles behind me was Raytown Station.

The well-worn tracks cut a clear swath through the trees and undergrowth. Looking up the tracks was like looking through a tunnel or into a canyon. Anyone walking along these tracks would be clearly seen. And so it was with Nellie. Brown and Reese saw her on these tracks and the confrontation ensued.

As I walked in the direction Nellie would have been traveling, I could not help but wonder what had been going through her mind. The threats...the whippings. Was she afraid for her life? If she was, why would she risk being alone here on these tracks? After all, Rafe had warned her that her tongue could get her in trouble. "Why" was the question I needed an answer for. Maybe I would find that answer in these woods.

"Over here, Mister Wood." Josiah was calling to me from the side of the tracks opposite from the pasture. He had found what looked like an old pig trail down through the growth. It was a tight fit, but we followed it for a short distance. "It was here, "said Josiah with his arms in an open gesture. "It was here where she was shot, and just a few steps to the east over there where she fell. Hard to tell with things grown up, but this fits the descriptions from the witnesses."

I don't know what I had expected to find. Don't know what I had expected a crime scene almost 20 years old to look like. But again, my thoughts went back to that July day when two men chased Nellie down that path and administered their final judgment. What that must have been like—for her and for them. The hunted, being taunted and pursued. The hunter loaded with pure evil.

I had seen enough and told Josiah we should take our leave to get back before dark.

CHAPTER 11

Wilkes County Courthouse
Washington, Georgia
October 6, 1865

"Captain Rundle, call your first witness," announced Commission President Western.

The time of judgment had come for Brown. He was about to face his accusers. Would his version of events be believable enough to spare him the gallows? I had to wonder what was going through his mind as Captain Rundle, the judge advocate, called his first witness, Nellie's son.

"Sir, I call Raphael West," responded Rundle as he faced the court-room, which had again had filled up with spectators and family members.

Capt. Thomas James Rundle, the government's prosecutor, was no stranger to military commissions. The 27-year-old New Yorker had recently led the successful prosecution of Edward Andrews in Orangeburg, South Carolina. Andrews got 10 years in prison for killing a colored man he believed had stolen his horse. Murder was the charge Rundle prosecuted, but the commission settled for a lesser charge of manslaughter.

Raphael West was young, but big and strong. His frame easily filled the chair that had been placed next to the commission's table for witnesses to use.

Rafe raised his right hand to take the oath, then planted himself in the old-fashioned, split-bottom wooden chair from which a parade of witnesses would testify. This was the second time he had been in front of Union soldiers and asked to take an oath to tell about the murder of his mother. Maybe this time would be easier.

"What is your name?" asked Captain Rundle.

"Rafe West," the lad responded.

He spoke softly, his words barely audible. "Speak up, son," Rundle admonished.

He gave a spirited response: "Yes, suh."

"Do you know the prisoners?" Rundle stepped aside so the witness would have a clear view of the defense tables.

"Yes, suh."

"What relation, if any, were you to the deceased woman, Nellie West?"

"I be her son," responded Rafe in a halting voice.

Rundle then asked the boy, "Is she dead?"

Rafe looked out into the courtroom, fixing his eyes on the family members, whose somber expressions were barely visible above the gallery railing.

"Yes, suh," he said softly with his voice dropping off. His eyes now looked down.

Captain Rundle fired a series of questions to the witness to reconstruct the events on the West Plantation the morning of July 13, 1865. From out in a field, a considerable distance away, Rafe had seen Brown confront his mother and loudly threaten her—threaten to "knock her damn brains out," Rafe recalled. He described seeing her leave the farm with the note to take to the federal soldiers. He went on to describe how he and his siblings found the mutilated body of their mother four days later.

"How long has Brown been your master or boss?" Captain Western, the chairman of the commission, asked.

"Goin' on five years, suh."

"Did he often use harsh treatment toward the workmen under his charge?" Western wanted to know.

"Yes, suh. Very bad."

Captain Rundle continued that line of questioning. "Did you ever see him use any harsh treatment toward your mother before the time on that Thursday morning?"

And Rafe firmly replied, "Yes, suh. I seen him use a lots a' hard treatment whit momma."

Then it was defense attorney Andrews' turn to question the victim's son. Drawing attention back to the morning Nellie left the farm, Andrews inquired whether Rafe's mother had said she wanted to stop by the field where the family members were working as she left.

"I hear her tell Massa Brown she wants ta go by da field on her way ta town. He say she should not, an' he wants her ta take da straight road, an' never wants her ta go to his field. If she do, he says some'ting 'bout 'portion' an' say he kill her."

And what about Reese, Andrews asked. "When Reese threatened her with the chair? Did he raise it?"

"He not raise it," Rafe said, "but were standin' near da chair."

By the time Raphael West completed his testimony, the commission members had a good sense of life on the farm and Brown's treatment of the negroes who worked there. Rafe had also given the commission an eyewitness account of events leading up to his mother's departure from the farm and the discovery of the body. However, only one witness could take them to the scene of the murder. And he would testify next.

A stir filled the courtroom when Captain Rundle announced to the commission that Christopher Reese, the co-defendant, would take the witness chair.

Andrews immediately rose to object to his being brought in to testify.

The military prosecutor quickly fired back: "I am of the opinion that the testimony of C.C. Reese is necessary to further the ends of justice, for which this commission has been convened, and without it the conviction or acquittal of one of the prisoners will depend altogether upon circumstantial evidence, which kind of evidence, I have authority for saying, is not very readily to be received by courts-martial or military commissions, when conviction of the accused depends upon that alone."

Captain Western agreed with the judge advocate that the commission would hear from Reese. "Bring the witness forward, captain," he ordered.

"Your honor!" Andrews rose from his seat again with an arm raised for recognition. "I must protest. Reese's being offered as a witness on the part of the prosecution, is objected to, on the grounds that he has been convicted of a felony upon his own voluntary confession of guilt; and also because the prisoner John M. Brown, who is charged as an accomplice, made a voluntary confession under promise of mercy by Brigadier General Wild, who received said confession!"

Captain Rundle rose from his seat to counter: "Although the accused, C.C. Reese, has pleaded guilty to the charge and specification against him, still he is as yet neither convicted nor sentenced for crime, and therefore the rule found in the Code of Georgia, S.3777 does not apply. In Wharton's American *Criminal Law* it will be laid down on page two hundred ninety-two that conviction without judgment works no inability to testify."

"As to the second point," Rundle continued, "I deny that the so-called confession of the prisoner Brown is a confession, for it lacks the one essential element which would make it admissible and admit the prisoner to clemency or pardon. Throughout the whole statement he takes care to make himself appear innocent and throw all the guilt on the other party.

"Again I am of the opinion General Wild had no authority to give a promise of mercy for voluntary confession; and even allowing that he had such authority, I deny that he, General Wild, did say anything to prisoner Brown until after he commenced to give his statement of his own free will, even were it a question which the prisoner should have been allowed to testify against the other."

Bringing his argument to a close, Rundle offered, "It is clear in my mind in view of the facts I intend to prove, that the testimony of C.C. Reese should be so received, for by other witnesses I shall corroborate his statement in many points, while by the same witness I will be able to prove the falsity of a part of Brown's statement."

Rundle had made his best effort to get Reese on the witness stand and proved himself quite the equal for the learned Andrews and Weems. But the decision now rested with the four members of the commission.

Following a brief conference, the commission dismissed Andrews' challenge and voted to hear from Reese, who was promptly called to be sworn in.

"What is your name and what is your age?" Rundle asked as he started his questioning.

"Christopher Columbus Reese; my age twenty," replied Reese.

"State the circumstances which occurred in the morning before Nellie left the place. Tell what Brown did and said, and what you did and said."

Rundle's question had the effect of opening a flood gate of damning evidence against Brown. But would the military commission buy Reese's story?

Reese talked about arriving at the Brown house before breakfast to find John and Nellie arguing in the yard. "Nellie had a handkerchief around her neck. He, Brown, caught hold of that handkerchief and choked her; was cursing her still…he told her he was going to send her to Washington, Georgia. He got me to write a note to Captain Cooley."

If Reese feared any retaliation for telling his story to the commission, he did not show it. His demeanor was cool; his words, calculated. Sitting erect in the witness chair, he continued to let his barbarous tale unfold.

"When she, Nellie, came in the house, I asked her where did she want to go; she did not tell me. I asked her again; I think she said she wanted to go home or something. I told her if she did not tell me where she wanted to go, I would slap her over. She then said she would go to Washington."

Reese explained that Nellie left the house, hobbling off down the main road with her note from him and some personal effects wrapped in that handkerchief. She hoped next she would come under the protection of the Union authorities in Washington. But that was not the outcome Brown wanted, according to Reese.

"After she had left, Mister Brown told me he would give five dollars that morning to see that damned old bitch hung."

Reese told how Brown suggested they go hunting, and while they were walking toward the railroad tracks, Brown talked about how he regretted allowing Nellie to go speak to the Union soldiers. Next Reese detailed the deadly confrontation with the woman on the tracks and described how Nellie ran to try to get away. Finally he took full responsibility for succumbing to Brown's repeated urgings and firing a fatal shot into the woman's back.

Once they were back on the plantation, Reese said, he and Brown spent an otherwise normal afternoon on the farm with visitors joining the family for dinner and an afternoon of hunting. Later that night, Reese rejected Brown's suggestion that they cut up the body so it would not be found.

Satisfied that his witness had sufficiently cloaked Brown with responsibility for the murder of Nellie West, Rundle turned his attention to Brown's actions after his arrest.

"State anything which occurred in the jail which relates to this case," Rundle said.

"While I was there in the jail in Augusta, Mister Brown went around with paper and pencil to see if he could get men to write anything they heard me say about the case."

But that was not Brown's first effort to gain information to sacrifice this young accomplice.

"And while we were in Washington jail, the time before this, he begged me to confess to the murder and told me it would be best for me. Said they would prove it on me anyhow. Kept after me until I did confess it."

Stepping toward Reese, Rundle pressed harder. He already knew the answer he wanted to hear. "State anything Brown said or proposed in Augusta about the case and about the witnesses."

Reese hesitated then looked over at Brown. "He told me he would give five hundred dollars if I would swear he had nothing to do with it."

The courtroom burst into animated protests. Clearly what Reese was selling was not being bought by the whites who were watching, especially Brown's family.

Captain Western rapped the gavel for silence. Then he proposed a question of his own for Reese. "Had you associated with Brown previous to the murder of Nellie?"

Reese turned his head to address his answer directly to Western. "No, sir. I had been home but about two years from the war before the murder took place. I think I had seen him twice at his house, once at a party there. I never was much with him."

Andrews had been taking copious notes while seated at the defense table with Brown and Weems. Now it was his turn to quiz the government's star witness. He slowly rose from his chair and locked eyes with Reese, who responded by fidgeting a bit in the chair, but quickly regained his composure.

As a former state jurist, Andrews knew what he was up against. He strongly objected to the administration of justice by military tribunals, which were composed of officers with no legal training. In fact, many officers served because they had no other pending assignments. Andrews now found himself precisely where he had long ago predicted the criminal justice system was headed: "I regret to say, that within my experience, I have noticed a decline, not only in the respect due, and once paid to the courts of justice, but, as a necessary consequence, of the law itself." He was about to put his observation to the test on behalf of his client.

"Mister Reese," he began, pacing in front of the witness chair. "Did you make confession of having killed Nellie West to anyone except when you confessed before General Wild? If so, state who the persons were, and where it was made."

Reese thought for a moment. "Yes, I told Schribner, a federal soldier in the jail here in Washington. I think it was four days after my confession was taken down by General Wild; it was the only confession I made before that, I recall."

Weems reached across the defense table and handed Andrews a wrinkled white sheet of paper. He began to recite from it a list of names.

"Did you not confess at different times to Wilson Brown, Mister Gagle in Augusta, Caroline Garrett and Miss Brown, a man by the name of Copeland, and a colored man named Moses Coleman, in Augusta, and the federal soldier by the name of Schribner, that Brown had nothing to do with the killing of Nellie West? That you did it yourself, and Brown was not to blame, or words to that effect; or, what did you say?"

Andrews knew well that jailhouses were full of loose lips. Information was the only commodity that prisoners had at their disposal. And they would use it liberally to gain favor with their cellmates and guards and others. Whether the words were true or not did not matter, until the prisoner got to court, where a lawyer could serve them up like the main course of a banquet.

"I never told any person that Brown had nothing to do with the killing of Nellie West." Clearly, Andrews had struck a nerve. Reese became quite agitated, and his words began to fall out more rapidly. "Neither did I tell Wilson Brown, Mister Cagle, Caroline Garrett, Miss Brown, nor Copeland, nor Coleman, that I did it myself, but I did tell Schribner, the federal soldier, that I did the deed. I have spoken only to Cagle. He called me to him and said that Brown had told him to tell me that if I would get him out of it, Mister Brown would get me out of it, meaning to get me out of the difficulty."

Andrews paused for a moment, reaching under his coat to adjust the thin black tie he wore over the embroidered collar on his white shirt. The time had come to pry deeper and raise the volume of his voice a notch for effect: "Did you ever tell Bud Pittman about killing Nellie West, in Taliaferro County, before you were put in jail in Washington; and if so, what did you say?"

"Yes, sir." Reese now became a bit more flustered. He slowed down his speech enough to consider carefully each word he was about to say. "I do not recollect what I told him. I told him I was very uneasy, and if he would not ever tell anyone, I would tell him—as he and I were great friends. He said he would not tell and then I told him something about me and Mister Brown killing a negro. Did not say who the negro was, that I recollect."

Andrews now stood fixed in front of Reese's defense table, blocking his view of his attorney. There would be no visual clues from Barnett to coach him as the questioning turned to the events at the West Plantation. "Where were you when you threatened her with a chair? And how often did you threaten Nellie?"

"I was in the house, standing close to the door, near the desk, when I threatened to slap her over. I never did threaten her with a chair, that I recollect."

Andrews held up a copy of Reese's statement. He referred to it as he asked him: "Did you tell on former examination about Brown choking Nellie, and that he would give five dollars to have her hung? If yes, when and where? "

"I think I did so state, but do not recollect distinctly."

Andrews pressed Reese, "Did you not swear in Augusta that Brown offered you five dollars to kill Nellie?"

Reese began moving nervously in the chair, craning his neck around to get a glimpse of Barnett, for the slightest of cues. "Do not know that I did."

Andrews' voice rose even louder. "Have you stated on any former examination at Washington or Augusta that you asked Brown why you were as deep in it as he; and if so, which examination?"

Reese lowered his head, "Do not recollect whether I did or not."

Andrews continued the assault. "Did you or not state in your examination before General Wild that Brown said the river bridge was a good place to kill the deceased?"

"I recollect saying something about one of the bridges as a good place to kill the deceased."

The memory lapses by Reese only fueled Andrews to probe even deeper. "Did you state in any previous examination that Brown said he would give you his daughter if you would kill the deceased?"

At that question, Reese's head popped up and his eyes locked on Andrews. His hands pushed on the arms of the chair, thrusting himself to his feet. The guards took a few steps in his direction. "I never said before that Brown promised his daughter if I would kill the deceased. I was very much excited, and there were many things I never thought of."

The air of expectation that had been building in the courtroom finally exploded. Several men in the spectator section rose to their feet, fists in the air and shouting. The negroes in the gallery joined the demonstration.

President Western gaveled the courtroom back to order and warned against any further protests. "Take your seat, Mister Reese," he told the defendant.

Andrews continued as Reese sat down, asking, "Did you tell Brown to fire on the deceased after you shot, and did you not so state on your former examination at Washington?"

"I do not remember whether I told Brown to fire or not. I do not remember if I so before stated."

"Did you state on any former examination at Washington anything about Brown's trying to get you to confess?

"I do not recollect whether I did or not."

Andrews was beginning to sense that Reese had said about all he wanted to say. However, he continued his questioning to make points with the commissioners as to Reese's credibility. About the only hope he had to save Brown was to attack Reese's veracity. "Did you ever state on examination before General Wild that Brown told you to take his gun and fire again at the deceased?"

"Do not think I did, but do not remember. There are a great many things I told them that I do not recollect."

Andrews referred back to the copy of Reese's confession that he was holding. "Did you not state before General Wild that you called on Brown twice to shoot deceased after you had shot her?"

"I think I did not so state."

Weems got up from the defense table and walked over to Andrews. The two men conferred for only a moment, and Weems returned to his seat. Reese looked over to his attorney, who nodded approvingly.

Andrews continued. "Did you not ask McLane, in prison in Augusta, if a man were to fire on or shoot a negro that had threatened him, what would be the consequence, or words to that effect, and what did you say to McLane on the subject?"

"I do not recollect what I said to him. There was something said about the case; I do not know what."

"Who confessed before General Wild—you or Brown?" Andrews now held the confession up close, examining it and running a finger along selected lines.

"Brown."

Dropping his hand that was grasping the papers to his side and leaning toward Reese, Andrews asked, "Did you not say this morning in jail, in the presence of Kennedy, if you were asked any more questions you were going to say you did not recollect, or words to that effect?"

"No, sir. I did not."

Andrews still had one more question. Returning to the murder itself, he asked: "Did you not swear in Augusta that you handed Brown the big granite rock and asked him to throw it, or words to that effect, and he refused?"

"I do not remember whether I did or not."

Whether the defense team scored any points that would help save their client from the hangman's noose was still unknown at this point. The commission members did look engaged. At least Andrews and Weems felt they had painted Reese as someone whose testimony could not be relied upon.

As Andrews returned to his chair, Captain Rundle followed the brutal cross-examination with a couple of his own questions. "What sort of feeling did Brown manifest when Nellie was killed?"

"He appeared to look as lively as ever," Reese replied, his memory returning.

Rundle then pressed Reese, saying, "Mention what occurred during the first examination in regard to your father."

"Father fainted on the floor," Reese replied rather matter-of-factly.

"Mister Reese?" Captain Western now joined in the questioning of the government's star witness. "Where were you arrested? Were you and Brown together?

"I was at Mister Pittman's at the time I was sent after. My brother came for me. I went to Brown's house and was there arrested. This was on Monday after Thursday when the killing took place. Brown was arrested on Sunday."

With the judge advocate and the defense team finished with their questions, the verbal sparring had come to an end for Christopher Reese. He was excused from the witness chair to return to his chair next to Mr. Barnett.

Had his testimony made an impact on the four commissioners? There was no doubt that the description from an eyewitness would bolster the government case, especially if that eyewitness were the perpetrator. Yet with as little as the witness yielded in his cross-examination, the defense team appeared encouraged.

———◆———

CHAPTER 12

Wilkes County Courthouse
Washington, Georgia
October 6, 1865

THE TRIAL PLODDED ALONG WITH a series of West family members testifying about the day Nellie was murdered and recounting their harsh treatment by Brown. Rundle was intent on exposing every flaw in Brown's character to demonstrate the way he manhandled negroes. William West knew about that treatment first-hand.

"We tooks holiday Thursd'y night," West testified, his young body shaking nervously. "Massa Brown promised holiday when we got da crop in. I went up ta him on Thursd'y night, an' told him we got along wit most of da field work, and told him we thank him fer da holiday."

Captain Rundle asked, "Did Brown say anything to you?"

"Suh, Massa Brown say he satisfied an' would give us one, an' he give us holiday on Frid'y and Sarad'y. Frid'y we worked our crops. An' some of us was looking then fer the dead body."

"And why did you think you were looking for a dead body?" Rundle inquired.

"Suh, da reason I 'spec we hunted were dat we thought something was bad wrong because Miss Nellie was old, an' one who never did visit much about, an' she never was absent much from the company. She were crippled in one of her knees an' one of her big toes was mighty near cut off—I think on the right foot."

William looked up toward the gallery where the family was seated. "I seen on Frid'y a passel of buzzards on da lower part of da place where I be working my crop. I goes over der into da swamp an' look all about dere."

"Tell us about moving the cows," the prosecutor urged.

"Suh, dem cows been runnin' in da old pine pasture fer ny on two weeks as near as I can recollect. On Frid'y mornin' Gabrel goes ta drive dem cows back to where dey were going in da old pine pasture. Massa Brown drove ole' Gabrel an' made him go ahead of the cows, an' drive 'em back an' puts 'em back in the stubble field above da big house."

"Missus Brown didn't want the cows in the stubble-field, did she?" Rundle asked.

William replied, "No, suh. She had Gabrel take da cows out of da stubble-field an' put into the old pine field because she say da weeds in da stubble-field made da milk bad."

"Did you say anything to Gabrel?"

"Suh, I told Gabrel he would find his momma somewheres on da back part of da plantation, dead, for da reason dat da cows been changed so sudden; an' as I tells him, he hunted an' sho' nuf found her."

Then Rundle asked, "Did Brown say anything about where Nellie was gone, and if so, where?"

"Suh, Massah tells me he give her a line to go hunt her a home. Missus Brown say Nellie was g'wine to Washington, an' from dere ta Massa Tom West, an' from massa's down ta ol' Massa Butler."

Nellie's 15-year-old niece, Julia, who was working in the cook house, described the explosive events she had seen on the West Plantation the morning of the murder.

On cross examination, Andrews asked her, "Did you swear before General Wild, that Brown told Nellie to take all her children, and that he would not let the children go? And that Nellie said to you, not in the presence of Brown, that she was going to tell the Yankees all she knew?"

Julia responded, "Suh, I don't know if'n I says before dat Massa Brown told aunt Nellie ta take all her chillen. I swore dat Massa Brown made Miss Nellie go into da house an' tell all she was goin' to tell da Yankees."

"Did you swear before General Wild that Brown said if she, Nellie, put her foot on the fence to go to where the hands were, he would kill her?"

"Yes, suh, I did."

Nellie's 14-year-old son, Gabrel, who eventually found his mother's body, was tending to the cows the morning after Nellie left.

Captain Rundle said, "Tell what Mister Brown said to you about changing the pasture the day after Nellie left."

"Suh, I chose da old field where da cows be going all week. Den Massa Brown tell me he rather dey go into da wheat-patch. But da cows, dey being so used ta goin' down ta da old pine pasture, when dey went out da gap dey started down toward da creek an' da pines. Massa Brown den cursed an' damned me. He say if I not turn dem cows back he would take up a stick and kill me...."

Gabrel and his sisters found their mother's body during their search near the old pine pasture. Rundle asked the boy, "Tell me where you found the body, and how it was lying."

"Suh, found momma da udder side o' da railroad from Massa Brown's house, 'bout two hunurt yards from da railroad, on da ground on her face wit her head to da sunset an' feet toward sunrise. A big pine tree at her head an' little pines all 'round. Head broken whit rocks. Two rocks near, both whit blood on dem."

Andrews pressed William on the change in pastures. "Did not Brown give as a reason for changing the cows that you could manage them better, as the negroes had a holiday, and you would have no help in getting them up? Or, what reasons did he give for the change?"

"Suh, he say he think dat I not want to be bothered with dem much, 'cause I had holiday," William responded. "I did not ask Massa Brown ta make da change for dat reason...."

The next family member on the stand was Nellie's daughter Kitty.

"State all you heard about the message Nellie sent to you on Thursday," Rundle said.

"Momma told me dat Massa Brown say she should take her all an' go away from dere, an' give her orders do not come by da field. She did want ta go by da field ta carry da key an' sees her chillen. As she could not go by da field, she say she wanted ta see me by 12 o'clock to give me her key. I looked fer momma til 12 o'clock an' never seen her."

"Did you hear anything that morning?"

"Suh, between 8 and 9 o'clock we hear'ed a gun fired in da direction of Mister Flint's. As Momma did not come as she promised, I went ta lookin' fer her on Frid'y mornin'."

"What did you find?"

"Suh, I seen her tracks on da other side of da bridge goin' toward da pasture an' followed in at da gate fer about ten steps. Through da gap was a sandbar an' I could not follow it any more. One track were a shoe track, an' the other were a boot track whit iron plate on one side of da sole-heel." Kitty looked over toward the defendant's table and hesitated. After a moment, she added, "Da shoe track were Massa Brown's track."

The gallery erupted in boisterous reaction. Rafe and a few others rose to their feet with their hands waving in the air. Others turned to hug their seatmates. Western gaveled the demonstration to order.

Captain Rundle continued. "State what conversations you had with Brown on Friday morning about Nellie."

"Suh, Massa Brown asked me where Rafe were. I tells him I do not know where he be. He say all of us wanted ta do like Momma done, kick up a rumpus, an' did not want ta stay dere an' work. An' he says, 'if any of you want to go off I will give you a note to go to the Yankees'—that's what he says, alright."

***

Liberty Hall
Crawfordville, Georgia
March 25, 1883

As I sat on the porch listening to Josiah recount the trial of Nellie West's killers, I was appreciative that he had used strategic moments to provide context. That was important to understanding the people involved and why they had acted the way they did. After all, he was here and had lived through the Reconstruction that I had only read about from afar.

"It really doesn't take much to scare the coloreds, to get them to do what you want," Josiah started. "Threats of whippings and beatings by the white overseers were rather predictable."

"How's that?" I wondered.

"You knew it was coming and how it would end. Straight up. No questions needed." He leaned forward in his chair toward me and lowered his voice a bit. "What really scared them was the tales of conjuring among themselves. And if they put enough faith in those stories, you can imagine what went through their minds when their white masters told them stories about what the Yankees would do to negroes."

Josiah leaned back, and I again put my pencil to paper. "Conjuring? I'm not sure I follow you."

"Witchcraft, voodoo, whatever you want to call it."

"But weren't these folks Christians? They did have their iterant ministers and praise meetings and such." I wasn't following the narrative.

"Let me explain."

"Please do," I responded, leaning back in my chair.

"Yes, they have Christian religion, but in the depths of their culture, there is another place. It's a place where bad things can happen, and if you believe the stories, actually do happen."

"What do you mean by 'bad things'?" I asked. "What's worse than being killed by Brown and Reese?"

"What's worse is the state the family found Nellie's body in. Picked apart by vultures and insects, and with bugs crawling over and into it. The fact that she died in a most brutal way."

"Yes?" I'm trying to follow along.

"A scene like that can bring to life the conjuring stories those West children have been hearing all their lives."

"Give me an example," I pleaded. I thought the homebrew had gone to Josiah's head.

"All right. This didn't come out at trial, but some of the family said the body had a silver coin tied to its leg. Silver money tied in such a manner is supposed to protect you from evil. Nellie obviously sensed danger was near, or she never would have done that. She was raised to believe that coin would protect her."

"And...." I urged Josiah to continue.

"The negroes believe if you put a silver coin in your mouth and it turns black, someone is plotting to hurt you. Again, Kitty later told the family that Nellie had put a coin in her mouth in such a manner and it turned as black as a cast iron skillet. And the vultures and bugs and insects crawling over the body are a visible sign to them that Nellie was cursed." Josiah paused for a moment and looked over at me. "That's conjuring."

"Or coincidence?" I found the description fascinating—but believable? Not at all.

"Mister Wood, I admit it's hard to grasp. This is so foreign to white people, but this is part of plantation life." Josiah could see I was still a bit puzzled by the subject.

"The West negroes testified in the white man's court in a manner that white people would understand. For sure, they didn't know whether Brown or Reese were conjuring up something for each of them even as the trial was under way."

"So, what might have happened to Kitty or William or the others? Or what did they think might happen?"

"We'll never know, but there was talk about a lot of strange things that happened to members of the family. One of the older members took sick after getting into a spat with Brown. They were convinced that Brown had cast a spell on the woman. She fought a fever for weeks. Family members said they saw spiders crawling out of the woman's nose and mouth. A doctor checked her and could not determine what ailed her. Then a couple of weeks later she died. And a snake crawled out of her forehead, sticking its tongue out at the family members gathered around.

"They also told about when Brown sent a black chicken to the quarters for a holiday meal. The thing clucked around outside the cabins, but nobody would touch the fowl for fear it was an evil sign. After a few days, a big knot popped up on the hen's head. The bird drooped around for a couple more days, then just up and died in front of Nellie's cabin. They say Rafe was the one who finally got close enough for a good look. He reported the boil on the hen's head had burst, and that convinced everyone the animal was poison. A few days later Nellie cut her right toe—nearly severed it—as she chopped some firewood."

"That's amazing for sure," I replied with a smile.

"Mister Wood, these tales from the coloreds do amaze us, but to them they are the God's honest truth." Stephens poked his index finger into his knee. "These stories scare the hell out of them, even more than the threat of a whipping. I think it's a real testament to them that they are willing to tell their stories in court."

CHAPTER 13

Washington, Georgia
March 26, 1883

I WANTED TO KNOW MORE about the place where the trial had been held, so I hopped the railroad for the relatively short ride north to Washington, Georgia.

The trip up was uneventful. I spent the ride in my green Pullman car reviewing notes I had collected from an earlier interview that I thought might be helpful. As we passed through Raytown station and alongside the West Plantation, I could not help but think about Nellie's killing. I strained for a glimpse of the murder scene out the right-side window. Couldn't see much. It had just been far too long and there was too much overgrowth. Nonetheless, I felt a chilling sensation as we rolled by near the pine field I had visited earlier with Josiah.

The railroad station in Washington was a healthy walk from the courthouse. Healthy and pleasant enough. Approaching the outskirts of the downtown, I passed Haywood, the home of Judge Andrews. The small plantation house sat some distance back off the main road, up on a slight rise. The setting was quite lovely.

I tried to get a sense of what this town was like in the post-war months of 1865. It wasn't that long ago. But the town now looked so different from the way I had imagined it after speaking with someone who was here at the time.

First settled as Heard's Fort, this region was a hotbed of revolutionary activity by the time the colonies had broken away from England. The patriot victory at the Battle of Kettle Creek is still a point of pride among townsfolk, I was told.

Wilkes County was one of the original seven counties organized in Georgia in 1777. Over the years, pieces of it would be taken to create additional counties, including Taliaferro. Agriculture was an important economic resource, and by 1860, 70 percent of the population were slaves.

During the previous conflict, the county seat, Washington, was an important crossroads for troops headed home from North Carolina. A few months before the end of the war, the Confederates had placed a pontoon bridge over the Savannah River at Lisbon—about 20 miles from here—making the trek a bit easier.

Some had come on horses and wagons, but many had walked. When they reached the city, they would sign loyalty oaths and continue home. Those with some money could complete the trip home by train. For most, though, reaching home would be a much longer walk.

Washington was also the nearest city for the freedmen in these parts to gather. Outside of Augusta, it was the only town of any consequence with a Union garrison to which negroes could take complaints or seek protection. For weeks and months after the surrender, veterans and former slaves alike had crowded into Washington, camping on the streets and public places, wherever they could find a spot.

The man who had been sent here to keep the peace as the city's first Provost Marshal was Capt. Lott Abraham, commanding Company D of the Fourth Iowa Cavalry. His soldiers and their horses had arrived by train from Macon, and the men set up camp near the same railway station where I had arrived.

In the weeks leading up to my trip to Crawfordville, I had occasion to meet with Abraham, who, now many years later, was farming 340 acres in Center Township, Iowa, with his wife, Sarah, and their four children. I found his now middle-aged frame topped with a mop of long gray hair. He was wearing the farmer's uniform of coveralls and tending to a small garden near his modest house. While in the army, he had kept his hair cut short but allowed for a small distinctive mustache, which he has kept over the years. Even now, Abraham has retained the solid build of a young soldier. That's what farming will do to you.

Abraham was just 27 when he assumed his first military assignment. He joined the Iowa cavalry as a private in November 1861 and within two years was wearing captain's rank. The men in his command had fought their way across Alabama to Georgia. Two members of the company received the Congressional Medal of Honor for actions in Selma, Alabama, and Columbus, Georgia.

During our discussion on his farm, he had a strong recollection of his time in Washington. I took copious notes and brought them with me on my trip to relate them to what I would be seeing first-hand.

The day was already heating up. I found a cool spot on a bench in the shade of an old oak on the courthouse grounds. Occasionally a gray squirrel would dart by in search of an acorn. Gray-feathered pigeons wandered up close to my feet while pecking the ground for seed snacks. I removed my hat, set it on the bench next to me and pulled the notes of my interview from my coat pocket.

Abraham had told me that his unit's journey to Washington actually began while the men were camped at Macon, Georgia. On Thursday, May 4, his headquarters received a telegram to send an officer and 50 men to Washington to parole some of Gen. Joe Wheeler's cavalry. "I got that assignment without asking," he told me. His company left out of Macon on the train to Atlanta, where they waited more than four hours "by the moonlight in the ruins of a city once so lovely" for the connection to Washington.

They finally arrived midafternoon on Saturday, two days later. He found Washington also was "a lovely town," he recalled. I could see that for myself on the walk to the courthouse. The buildings surrounding the square showed much activity. It was easy enough to tell the farmers from the city folk. I observed even the whites and coloreds now shared the same sidewalks without conflict. Abraham remarked how strange it was to see Rebel soldiers in their gray uniforms carrying their Enfield rifles and crowding the rail station when he arrived. My arrival had been less dramatic, and the folks in the streets were moving at a most leisurely pace.

"My men got right to work guarding government warehouses and giving paroles. They call them 'payrolls,'" recalled the captain, chuckling at the play on words. I tried to visualize the picture he was painting for me of a "lovely town" in a chaotic environment. He went on to tell me that the evening of his arrival, he rode out of town to a camp to receive the surrender of General Lewis and an entire brigade of Rebels—the Kentucky Orphan Brigade. They stacked their weapons, and Abraham, who held court under a big tree, signed papers until midnight.

The Iowans set up their office in town—in the courthouse, no less, the very building where in a few months General Wild would conduct his interrogations and a military commission later would hold a murder trial. But Abraham didn't spend much time in the office. He said he was constantly on the move to meet arriving units to issue paroles "until late at night, hardly stopping to eat."

He enjoyed talking with the former Confederate soldiers and learned from them that Jeff Davis had passed through Washington a month earlier. And his wife had come through a bit earlier than her husband.

The work assigned to the soldiers was quite burdensome, he told me. "I must work without ceasing for here they come in squads and shag lines hunting their 'payrolls.'"

But the soldiers were not the only people demanding attention from the occupation forces. "Citizens flock in to ask questions and tell what they have suffered," Abraham said. "But the negro occupies the biggest corner of their hearts, and generally what comes out first is the question 'Are you going to set them free?'

"Oh yes," he would tell the white folks. "They're freed long ago," he would explain.

"But what will become of them?" They want to know about the negroes. "They'll all die, starve to death or steal all we have or kill us." The people of Washington were clearly concerned, and even more afraid of the unknown that lay ahead. This was the context in which John Brown was keeping his negroes under his thumb on his plantation, even to the extent of making them get permission notes from him to leave the property.

"I could tell them only that I had no idea what kind of being the African is," I remember Abraham telling me. "The whites, they spoke nonsense. They spoke of negroes as everything but human, no good in any respect."

In the days ahead the Rebels began arriving in town in greater numbers, filling the courthouse square and every public space available. Generals Vaughn and Debrill arrived with about 2,400 well-mounted cavalrymen ready to record their paroles, giving Abraham one of his biggest challenges.

I could visualize the soldiers atop their horses, moving along the main street in Washington. A sea of gray uniforms in various states of repair. A formation of proud, but defeated, Confederates, seen in this manner for perhaps the last time.

These were the same troops that had provided escort for President Davis as he fled into Georgia ahead of advancing Union forces. But by the time they reached that pontoon bridge over the Savannah River at Lisbon they had broken from the president's party because of the inevitability of Southern defeat. The members of this escort were among the few Confederates who actually got paid for their service—about $23 each.

For a while, a tense standoff developed between the newly arrived Rebels and the severely outnumbered Iowans. "They refused to surrender to me and stack arms," as Abraham described the moment. "I had not the men to confront them to do it. I got General Vaughn to consent to go to Augusta with me. He took part of his staff and...I took an orderly. We had a pleasant ride.

"We met General Upton at the hotel. I laid the case before him and introduced General Vaughn. A telegraph was sent to General Wilson and we waited. To bide the time, I took a stroll over into South Carolina by moonlight." When Abraham returned to the hotel, the answer awaited him. He was advised that those of General Vaughn's men who could not go home by rail could keep their horses. Conflict averted!

Robert Toombs had a big house just down the street from the Washington courthouse. It stood stately, back on the lot, two stories high, big columns rising in the front. Very appropriate for the former Confederate Secretary of State and General Officer.

Abraham recalled one day when Toombs came to his office. "I talked with him a while then went down to his house. I took a lieutenant and two other men with me and counted five thousand, one hundred eighty dollars in specie that he says Breckenridge threw down in front of his gate. Toombs said the general told him they had more than they could carry, mostly silver.

"It took some time to count it then. I gave the old fellow a receipt for it and took a drink with him."

I'm still learning that an important part of Southern hospitality is a good, stiff drink.

"He talked very fast and he asked me what was the reason they gave me no orders to arrest him? He thought it ought to be done, but the general ought to have said so. Certainly, he knew Toombs was here." Abraham has no answer for the portly secessionist. For the moment at least, Toombs' status did not matter to the local Yankee commander.

That would change just three days after their meeting, Abraham said. "Captain Saint came up drunk to arrest Toombs and let him escape." And escape he did, all the way to Europe, leaving his wife behind.

Abraham kept returning to the mass of soldiers who were congregating in Washington. "The town was full of many armed Rebel soldiers, but they seemed to be backward about beginning a fight. I tried to prevent them from getting whiskey. They'd go off and fire a few shots."

The Union soldiers, meantime, were gathering up the property of the former Confederate government and sharing it with freedmen and other poor people. "The citizens began to act a little better toward me," Abraham observed.

Seizing on what he thought were good feelings, he attended Sunday services in the Methodist church. The captain recalled how sulky some of the congregation looked.

"The rebel preacher, Rev. Habersham J. Adams, couldn't look at me and couldn't say what he wanted to." Abraham said, "Hoping for change in attitude, I went in the evening again and felt frustrated."

I later learned how Reverend Adams came to pastor that church. He followed Rev. W. A. J. Fulton to the pulpit. Fulton had driven the church into very poor condition by the end of the war. And it didn't take long to find out why. Fulton was found to be an imposter who had married several women and deserted them. His church credentials were also false. He fled Washington for the safety of the federal troops in Milledgeville. But that's another story.

I continued to shuffle through my notes as I took in the sights and sounds of Washington from my bench on the courthouse grounds. The songbirds in the trees above me provided the musical accompaniment. Captain Abraham's words were coming to life for me. It was so easy to envision this place and its people in those tumultuous post-war weeks and months.

In my notes, Abraham went on: "I recalled one evening I got a dinner invitation from Mister Marcus, a jolly old Jew. His residence was south of town. I got a good dinner and stayed with him two hours. I left with an invitation to call often and come live there if I wanted."

And for entertainment? "One evening Mister Franklin, one of the lieutenants and I came up to town and looked in at a negro dance where they were dressed in style and danced like as though they got paid for it. I had too much curiosity at such times."

Abraham said on May 24, his Iowans left Washington "rather reluctantly" for Atlanta, only to return a few days later. When they got back, an infantry captain was serving as provost marshal. Abraham found the citizens still "had many questions to ask and complaints to make against the poor negroes, though their work went on well enough so far as I could see. I didn't see much friendship among the citizens. Just foolish people."

Provost marshal duty in Washington had become rather predictable. Issue pardons, answer questions, maintain order. So Abraham was not prepared for the events of June 4. For on that day he heard much conversation of a great robbery of gold and silver, in an amount approaching a half million dollars. Recalling the events, Abraham told me he "communicated with General Winslow and investigated his suspicions of a great treasure somewhere."

With the help of former Confederate Gen. E. Porter Alexander and some of the local boys, Abraham was able to recover some of the money. He said his men took "possession of one hundred six thousand, two hundred eighty dollars in gold and silver and put it in the bank." It's a number that Abraham even today doesn't have to think about. Just rolls off his tongue as he tells the story.

The soldiers then set out for Danburg, northeast of Washington, up toward the Savannah River. "We made ready for a trip and slept until 10 o'clock at night, then went all night," he recalled. "We were summoned to Reverend Chenault's house just at daylight Monday and caught the band of robbers. They surrendered very reluctantly, and we took their arms." To hear him tell it, the hunt was far from over. "I left them under guard and went on hunting for others. I returned at noon to find the worst ones gone—the guard in the broad daylight let such men escape. We returned to Washington out of humor."

That was some adventure the Iowans were involved in, and how frustrating it must have been to have their captives escape. But this was not the end of Abraham's angst, as I soon learned.

"All went on swimmingly, but the bank representatives and robbers all came back to Washington that evening, released by General Winslow. I gave up the money. No help." The search was over for now, at least as far as the military was concerned. As frustrating as it was, the whole affair wasn't a total loss for Abraham and one of his lieutenants. They kept two of the robbers' fine black horses. And a month later, as I later learned, General Wild took up the investigation of what happened to the rest of the loot.

On June 13, Company D of the Fourth Iowa Cavalry for a second time concluded its assignment in Washington, rolling out of town on the 9 a.m. train for Atlanta. But again they were called back. "The general gave me an order to go back to Washington with my company and stay there," said Abraham.

When I returned, "I found a new officer, Captain Cooley, and fifty men of the 156th New York there to relieve Captain Sheafer. All's well and I got a room at Dr. Heard's. A good room and attended church over Sunday." Abraham enjoyed his time visiting "the country people" as he called them, people he admitted were "getting very clever."

Again he received orders to deploy his unit to Atlanta, this time to head back to Iowa—to be mustered out of service "and to let the infantry have this place." But Abraham delayed the departure for a few days. He had one final bit of business to which he needed to attend.

"I had an interesting time trying to get some Rebel ladies to make me a U.S. flag. Missus Norman was first to refuse. Then her friends, then others. Missus Heard had to make it." After four years of fighting, perhaps the ladies had just forgotten what the flag looked like? I was willing to give them the benefit of the doubt. No matter. Abraham got his flag.

"The old flag went up high on the courthouse," he recalled with pride, "but I could not be there to see it because I was hunting old Toombs. Rode fifteen miles at night and searched Chenault's house at daylight again, then off into the swamps. But soon found our little guide 'Wilkes' knew but very little about the country or anything else. Made a big ride and returned to town before night. Tired. Mad. Finally resolved to bother myself no more in the country on such business."

It didn't help matters that the townsfolk held a community meeting on June 24 for the purpose of developing better relations with the occupying army. Judge Andrews tried to be the peacemaker, helping to pass such resolutions as the one thanking the Union troops for their "courteous and considerable conduct." But relations didn't get better. They got worse.

On July 1, Abraham and his Iowans finally left Washington and headed home. Washington now became the responsibility of Capt. Alfred Cooley and the New York Colored Troops. The townsfolk would find Cooley was no pushover. His bravery had been on full display on the battlefield at Cedar Creek. For it was on that field when several of the color guard had fallen to fierce firing, that Cooley charged into the maelstrom to strip the regimental colors from its staff and return it to safety. In that fight alone, the New Yorkers would lose 92 men to death, wounds and capture.

The Fourth of July was a day of celebration in Washington—celebration for the soldiers and the freedmen. Gunfire salutes from the soldiers and a massive picnic for the negroes at the formerly all-white gathering place known as Cool Springs made it a festive time. The local white citizens stayed away, preferring not to socialize with "Lincoln's rats," as the Union troops were known. Two days later the locals held their own "Rebel 'cue," but the hot weather and observant Yankee soldiers put a damper on what they had hoped would be an equally joyous affair.

Hostilities lingered, and when the Union soldiers left altogether in the fall of 1865, outlaws turned to shooting, burning and beating the negroes.

———◆———

Before taking my leave, I wanted to visit the rooms in the courthouse where the interrogations and trial had taken place. I tucked my notes away, put on my straw hat and headed up to the main entrance of the two-story red brick courthouse with its distinctive bell tower.

Only in my imagination could I even attempt to get an understanding of what had been feeding the cauldron of dissent in these parts in the summer of 1865. Captain Abraham may have found it to be a "lovely place," but the scars of discord cut very deep, as Nellie West so sadly discovered.

———

CHAPTER 14

Liberty Hall
Crawfordville, Georgia
March 27, 1883

WITH JOSIAH'S GOOD MEMORY, I was never far from the story I was beginning to embrace more eagerly.

"Folks from all around these parts are focused on the trial. People are talking about it everywhere, especially among the freedmen. But on this particular day, right slap in the middle of the trial, something happens that will have significant consequences."

For the life of me, I could not fathom what Josiah was talking about. Seems to me the biggest consequences would be the sentences these men got.

"You seem to have forgotten lesson number one, Mister Wood?"

"I have?" Where was he going with this?

"Sir, you have forgotten your instruction on justice in the South."

"How so?" I asked.

"Nothing is as it seems," Josiah responded with great confidence. "And this case is about to get its dose of politics. The stage for that was set on October 13th."

"How's that?" I asked, pressing for an answer to this mystery.

"That's the day Alexander Stephens got his parole from the President and began his journey home from Fort Warren."

Okay, now my editor's motive in assigning me to this project was becoming clear. One of the icons of Southern politics was in some way tied into the case of the murder of an old, feeble negro. I could not wait to see how this evolved, and I pressed Josiah to tell me more.

"So the day Uncle is released is the same day the prosecution rested its case. Now, we'll see just how clever Andrews and Weems can be to prove Brown's innocence."

"And how Alexander Stephens will help them," I thought.

———————

Wilkes County Courthouse
Washington, Georgia
October 13, 1865

For three months, John Brown had been protesting his innocence. Now he would get a chance to try to prove it before a court of law—a military court, no less. With a jury of his peers in a state court, Brown might have stood a better than even chance. But that is not possible in the current state of affairs.

Garnett Andrews called his first witness to the chair for examination. It was Jimmy Garrett, far from a disinterested bystander—Brown's stepson. Approaching his mid-30's, Jimmy was quite the experienced farmer, serving as an overseer on another plantation. He was tall and slim, with hair swept back behind his ears. Below his right eye was a scar—a reminder of how dangerous the careless use of farm tools could be. At least that's what they said. Some folks said the scar would better fit a kitchen knife in the hand of an unhappy wife.

Andrews opened his questioning by asking, "How long have you known Brown; what is his habit—swearing, blustering, and threatening negroes…?"

"I have known Brown some fifteen years." Garrett shuffled a bit in his seat, trying to get more comfortable, or was he just nervous? "He is a very blustering man…has been very wicked. I have frequently heard him threaten to knock their brains out. I have heard him say," Garrett started to wiggle his head a bit to imitate his stepfather, "'If you don't go and do so, you damn some-of-a-bitch, I will burst you open with something.' I have never known him to carry any of his threats to kill into execution, and I have been about his house a good deal."

Andrews pressed on, as Garrett struggled to get comfortable in the witness chair. "Is it anything uncommon for overseers and others managing negroes to make such threats, and when heard, do you expect them to be carried into execution?"

"It is not uncommon, nor do I expect the threats to be put into execution. It is not generally so expected. I have heard threats to burst open and kill all my life, and never know of any being executed."

Garrett let out a brief sigh, thinking the worst of the questioning was over.

"Mister Garrett." Captain Rundle addressed him as he approached the witness chair. "Was Mister Brown in the habit of stripping negro women naked to whip them?"

Garrett hesitated. "I have seen Mister Brown strip them of every garment to whip them."

Chairman Western interrupted with a question. "How long have you been an overseer?"

"About seven years before the war," replied Garrett, looking over at the panel of officers.

Chairman Western followed up, asking, "Did you consider it necessary to strip negro women to punish them?"

"I believe in living up to instructions. I was told by owners not to cut negro cloth all to pieces to get at their flesh, and I obeyed the orders."

Garrett's concern for preserving the clothing the negroes wore was somewhat driven by the small amount of clothing they were given. Slaves typically got clothing twice a year—once in the winter and again in the summer. Women would get dresses and aprons and sometimes undergarments. Men received shirts and trousers.

Before Garrett could step down, the prosecutor had one more question. "Did you tell Mister Brown on Thursday morning you were glad to find him out of a scrape? That you had been very uneasy about him and expected to find him in a difficulty now since you heard the negros were set free, knowing his temper?"

"No, Sir," Garrett replied firmly. "I never told him any such thing."

Caroline Garrett, Jimmy's sister and Brown's stepdaughter, unwittingly had as much to do with this murder as either of the accused. After all, she was offered up by Brown as the prize to Reese for killing Nellie. And the young Reese must have seen the older woman as one fine prize to risk his life for her. Curly hair cascading over her shoulders. Inviting sharp blue eyes. Curvaceous figure. Caroline would definitely have been a hormone trap.

As she recounted her jailhouse conversation with Reese, Andrews asked her, "Do you know anything of Rafe West and his mother—of their having a difficulty about that time, and what threat of violence did he make toward her?"

Caroline wasted no time getting straight to the answer. "On the Saturday before the fourth Sunday in June, Rafe and his mother having had a difficulty, and Rafe said he would split her damned brains out with a piece of light wood if she fooled with him."

Located in the country where the closest neighbor could be a half mile away the Brown farm infrequently had visitors. But a sometimes visitor was A. W. Barrett, who was asked by Andrews about a conversation he observed between Brown and Sam, one of the negro farmworkers who earlier testified to being savagely beaten.

Barrett looked over at the commission members and told his story. "...I was at a supper there and witnessed an interview between him and Sam. On the day previous a difficulty had occurred—Sam refused to do his work as Mister Brown had directed. Brown sent a little negro boy for two or three ash switches, this year's growth. Before Mister Brown had struck him, or before the switches were sent for, Sam had bit the hand or arm of Brown when Brown took hold of Sam. Brown...struck Sam twice, and the switches flew all to pieces."

Brown's trouble with Sam had not ended there. Barrett continued: "Sam on Sunday morning came to town to report to the officers. Brown ascertained that Sam had gone to town, and he came to my house and we agreed to go to town together to see what the difficulty would amount to. I was away from home and stopped at Brown's house before Brown returned. His family told me what he wanted and begged me to stay. While I was sitting at the supper table, Sam arrived and had a note which the officer in town had sent to Brown.

"When Brown looked and found what it was, he laid down his knife and fork, I think, and appeared in a very great passion. Was about to get up, when I spoke, and also his wife and I think his stepdaughter attempted to quiet him. I then read the note and told him there was nothing harsh or rough in it."

Andrews asked, "Then what did Brown do?"

"He got up and went to the door; first he stood and talked there, and I think sat down and lectured Sam some time. I thought it was a very appropriate lecture. After he was through, he told him to go to his house and Sam went off."

"Does or does not Brown curse, scold, and threaten negroes under him very much?" Andrews asked.

"He does," Barrett replied. "I have heard Brown threaten to kill, have heard him threaten to knock their heads off, to stamp their entrails out and so forth. Such language is very common among overseers. I never apprehended any difficulty when I heard such threats as to killing." Then he added, "I have many times made threats of killing without any intention of doing so."

Andrews asked again about the episode with Sam. "Did you come to town with Brown the next day, and was he punished for his treatment of Sam?"

"I came with him. He reported to an officer, a lieutenant, in command. I think the provost was absent in Augusta." Barrett paused for a moment and shifted in the witness chair. "Brown was not punished."

Standing at his desk, Captain Rundle asked, "Is it a general feeling among overseers that the killing of a negro would be a small affair when compared with the killing of a white person?"

In a very straightforward way, Barrett replied, "Not when under similar circumstances. This is my idea of the matter."

Captain Western had one question of his own before the witness was dismissed. "Is it customary when punishing negroes to whip them naked?"

"Partially naked. I mean it was as often done that way as any other," said Barrett nervously. Clearly, he was uncomfortable with the question and quickly added, "It was not customary to take all the clothes off. It was sometimes done."

John Brown's rotund brother, Tom, was the next witness for the defense. Took a few moments for him to fit himself into the witness chair. But, once Brown was settled, Andrews asked him, "Have you had any interview with Reese since in jail about his guilt, and the innocence of Brown, of the charge under which they are confined?"

"I have," the sibling replied. "I do not remember the date, sometime in July, just before they were sent off to Augusta. He said my brother did not have any hand in doing the work, that he did it himself. Also said if he had minded what my brother said, he would not have been in difficulty—and he begged him not to do it."

The defense continued its parade of witness who swore they didn't believe Brown had anything to do with Nellie's murder. One of Brown's former employers, John West, was asked about Brown's performance when he had worked as his overseer.

"How long did you employ Brown and did he whip much?" Andrews asked, adding, "Did you ever know him to strip a woman entirely naked to whip her?"

West replied, "...I believe three or four years...I was only at the place about three weeks during the whole year at different times. I don't think I ever saw him whip a negro. He might have done so when I was absent." As for his former employee's demeanor, West said, "Brown was noisy and boisterous about getting the hands up. I don't know that I ever knew him to curse. The negroes never made any complaints to me....he made good crops, and I considered that he got along with the negroes."

Then Captain Western inquired, "Had you known of your overseer stripping a woman naked to whip her, would you approve of it?"

"I would not," West replied. "I never heard of a case where a negro was stripped entirely naked. I think it would turn a man off who did so. Planters would not generally approve of it. I think they would be disgusted with the overseer who committed the act and the owner who allowed it to be done."

Andrews now reached the point in his presentation of evidence that he needed to hear directly from Reese's attorney, Samuel Barnett. Andrews wanted to use the defense attorney's testimony to discount a number of government arguments: that Julia did not swear in an examination before Wild that when she met Nellie, Nellie said she was going to tell the Yankees all she knew; that Brown threatened to kill Nellie if she went over into a field where the hands were; nor that Brown said he did not care a damn for the Yankees.

Captain Rundle objected to the defense ploy, saying written testimony could be produced, and those writings would be a higher authority than the recollection of attorney Barnett, or any other witness who might have been present when the former evidence was given. Further, Rundle argued the written statement could not be presented to the commission unless it be received as evidence, and then, the entire document must be presented, not just a part of it.

Captain Western agreed with the judge advocate and ruled that Barnett could not testify to the matters the defense requested, and that partial written testimony would not be accepted.

The ruling was a setback for Brown's case, but his attorneys had other questions for Barnett and dove right in. "Did not Reese know, before sworn, that you intend applying to the President for his pardon, and that a petition was getting up among his friends for that purpose?"

"I presume that Reese did know of the fact, though I have never told him of it," Barnett replied, looking over at his client. "It is a fact that a petition was getting up among his friends for his pardon."

"A petition" is putting it mildly. While Barnett was testifying, petitions were being circulated in Washington, Crawfordville, and other places asking for mercy for Christopher Reese. The testimony was not finished; the trial was far from over. But Reese's defense was already building a political case to spare the young man from the gallows.

Andrews continued, "Are you not employed by Reese, or his father, to prosecute Brown?"

"I am not employed to prosecute Brown," Barnett stated, "but in defending Reese, the prosecution is incidental, so in that sense I am engaged in the prosecution of Brown."

Andrews pressed on, "Was not the evidence taken before General Wild used in Augusta on an inquiry before Captain Malinda, and how long were we engaged in that inquiry?"

"It was used," Barnett replied. "We got through in one day. There were four or five additional witnesses examined. Copeland and McClone, James Garrett and Mister J.W. Reese and C.C. Reese, I think were all the witnesses who were examined."

Curious about what they were talking about, Western asked, "What was the cause of the inquiry made in Augusta?"

"A proposition to relieve Mister Brown from arrest. Commissioners heard testimony for that purpose," Barrett replied.

When Barnett yielded the witness chair and returned to his client's side, the defense presented another former employer of Brown's.

Judge Andrews asked, "You are Thomas B. Burdette?"

"I am," replied the man in the coat and tie, his dress quite in contrast to that of the other witnesses.

"Are you acquainted with John M. Brown's management of negroes? State whether or not he was cruel to negroes and whether you ever saw him whip one."

Burdette replied, "He lived on the place two or three years; I think now, four or five years. I was acting as agent for Mister West, and was over on the place frequently, sometimes two or three times a week, sometimes not so often as a week or two."

"And what did you observe?"

"I do not recollect that I ever saw him whip but one negro. One ran away and came to me. I took him home, and Brown gave him a light whipping. As soon as he commenced whipping, the negro made fair promises and he let him off. I do not think he was cruel to negroes. If he had been, I do not think he could have stayed in the place."

Andrews then asked, "From your knowledge of Brown as an overseer, do you believe he ever stripped one naked to whip her?"

No sooner was the question out that Rundle rose and immediately objected. "What Mister Burdette believes has no bearing on what Mister Brown actually did."

"The objection is sustained," announced Captain Western. Andrews turned to the president, saying, "Allow me to rephrase that." He turned back to Burdette. "Would you say that stripping a negro woman naked to whip her would be cruel?"

"I certainly think such a thing would have been cruel, and I think it would have come to my knowledge if it had been done. Mister West would not have kept Brown if he had known him to have been very cruel."

Rundle then asked, "How would the act of stripping negro women naked to whip them be regarded by planters generally?"

"I think it would not be tolerated by any man in my section of the country," Burdette responded. "I have never heard of a man being so stripped, much less a woman."

With Burdette taking his leave from the witness chair, Andrews and Weems submitted the statements taken by General Wild into evidence, including Wild's own statement recommending leniency for Brown for turning state's evidence. Then they rested their case.

Brown never took the witness stand in his own defense. A smart tactic? Perhaps. Perhaps not. The stakes would have been much different from the circumstances under which he had previously given a statement to General Wild. This time he would have been under oath, and his version of events would have been under direct challenge by a skilled prosecutor. No, with as big a mouth as Brown had, it was best in this case to let others talk for him.

———————

CHAPTER 15

Wilkes County Courthouse
Washington, Georgia
October 19, 1865

THE FOUR MILITARY OFFICERS SITTING in judgment of two civilians had, over the past two weeks, heard from a litany of witness about the brutal murder of an aging, crippled negro woman—a woman for whom the shackles of a lifetime in slavery had been broken only three months prior with the defeat of the Confederacy.

The trial of Christopher Reese and John Brown hinged not so much on the accounts of dozens of witnesses, both white and colored, but on the believability of the only two men who were present at the murder.

Garnett Andrews, a veteran of decades in the legal profession, both as lawyer and judge, now had the onerous task of pleading before the panel for the life of John Brown. How would he excuse away the damning testimony that put Brown at the center of this murder and exposed his history of brutality?

Andrews rose from his chair at the defense table. He momentarily hesitated. Ran his hand through his curly, graying locks of hair. Looked down at his client, who was somber and somewhat forlorn. Then over to his co-counsel, who gave an approving nod to begin his closing argument.

Andrews quietly turned his eyes to the commission members, acknowledging each officer individually with an engaging glance. Then, he spoke.

"Sirs, a professional experience of forty years has taught me that prisoners accused of very atrocious crimes are more easily convicted when…jurors, who, determining that blood must be had, have convicted on insufficient evidence…."

Years in the courtroom had taught this country lawyer that there was an easy way out for those sitting in judgment. He had seen it many times before. The challenge today was to convince the commission that conviction was not the easy way out for them.

Andrews continued: "And let me admonish the court lest under similar influence, they make a fatal mistake." He began slowly pacing in front of the table where the members sat. "There must be a motive for the commission of crimes, and the theory of this, by the prosecution, is that Brown had Nellie murdered because she would come to town and report him to the provost marshal."

He paused for a moment to let that statement hang before them. Then he set out to characterize Nellie's plans to see the authorities as nothing of any consequence, given Brown's own statements about it.

"Brown could have had no apprehension that such an extreme and criminal step was necessary, for Sam had been punished ten times worse than Nellie. He had reported to the provost marshal, and Brown suffered no punishment. Besides, Brown was alive to the great peril of such a deed, for when speaking of the accusation made by Ralph—that he had murdered his mother—he said he did not commit such crimes in good times, much less now, when they are so difficult."

It was nonsense, Andrews wanted them to think, that Brown would have hurt anyone in such circumstances. He walked over to the defense table to stand behind Brown, who did not stir, and placed a hand on his shoulder.

"If he had intended to murder her, he would not have sent her up to the railroad, the most public place in the neighborhood. He would have let her go by the cornfield, where she might have been shot down in some secret place."

No, Andrews was saying there was nothing his client said or did that even hinted at setting the woman up for murder.

Andrews now cast a gaze toward the judge advocate. "Says the prosecution, there were numerous threats made by Brown." Andrews' head pivoted back in the direction of the commission. "Now, in the first place, there were none made on account of Nellie's leaving. All were made before. Brown knew she was going to leave, and on account of her refusing to work, so far from threatening and murdering her for leaving, she went pursuant to his orders and wishes, as proven by Ralph, Caroline West and others.

"Secondly, we prove by other witnesses that such threats amount to and prove nothing." Andrews tossed his arms into the air and lowered his voice. "Barrett, Acree, their own witness, and others testify that such threats by men of his calling are no consequence whatever, that they never knew a negro killed in pursuance of them. It seems Brown threatened to kill everyone, but killed none."

The packed courtroom suddenly came alive with turning heads, exchanged glances and whispers. In the gallery, the negroes sat in stunned silence, trying to understand what was playing out before them.

Andrews pivoted toward the gallery and pointed his finger at Rafe, who was seated in the front row behind the railing. He was hunched over with his elbows on his knees and his chin in his hands. "Ralph threatened to knock his mother's brains out with a piece of light-wood." Rafe shook his head in response. Andrews turned back toward the commission members. "If such threats mean anything, then he should be under suspicion in his mother's death."

He continued, "Brown is charged with aiding and abetting the murder of Nellie. All the choking, threats, and so forth was a distinct act—a punishment for not washing. No murder could have been in contemplation until after Nellie left the house...."

The commission members had been admonished by Brown's learned counsel not to make a conviction the easy way out, but instead to understand that Brown had no intention to murder Nellie. And, a vigorous attack on the gunman himself would advance that argument.

"Reese's confession is that Brown instigated him to do the deed. Brown's is that it [the deed] was done against his remonstrance. Juries will not convict on evidence of an accomplice, though unimpeached, unless corroborated by other evidence, and in cases where there is no evidence to the contrary. We shall directly impeach the evidence of Reese. You have Brown's evidence before you contradicting it, and under these circumstances, there should be more than corroboration."

Andrews reached down to his table and picked up a sheet of paper. He put on his silver wire-rimmed eyeglasses and gave the paper a quick scan.

Looking up toward the commission, he resumed his argument. "As to Brown's aiding and abetting murder, it is known only to him and Reese, and one is as much entitled to belief as the other."

Again, he scanned his notes. "Now, after they left the house, and until the dead body was left in the woods, who but Reese gives any evidence of Brown's aiding and abetting the murder? We presume the argument of the prosecution will be that they started out with the common intent to murdering Nellie, and, first, that hunting squirrels was a pretext…."

Now Andrews began to pick apart the conflicts in the testimony. "Perhaps the prosecution may hold that Reese is corroborated by Raphael West, who saw Brown's track in the cane patch. Brown, the overseer, would make his tracks all over the plantation, including the cane patch. If Raphael is to be believed about the tracks, Reese cannot be. Reese swore that he and Brown kept to the big road up to the crossing, walking on the grass as much as they could. This contradiction may impair the credit of Raphael, so as not to be believed. If Reese is not believed, his case falls to the ground…."

The defense knew the key to making Brown's version of events credible was to destroy the believability of Reese's story. And Andrews continued his attack.

"Reese has as great an incentive as any witness could have to swear so as to convict Brown, for he not only had a motive for revenge upon Brown for having betrayed him, but as he is making efforts for a pardon, he knows that his chances will be better in the event Brown is convicted.

"According to Brown's statement," again Andrews refers to his sheet of notes, "Reese had a motive for shooting her, for like a rash and thoughtless young man, he had snapped a cap at her. He said that she would come to the Yankees and say he had attempted to murder her, which would have been almost as bad as killing her."

Jailhouse talk will always come back to haunt a prisoner, and for Reese that was no exception. His loose talk to the guard and Brown's relatives was seized on by Andrews.

"Brown's innocence was proven by the confession of Reese to three witnesses. Reese in his confession to Schribner says expressly that Brown had no hand in this killing, evidently intending that he was not responsible for it, as he himself makes a distinction between the mere physical acts which caused the death and the idea of killing, by which he means to include all circumstances tending to and aiding in the act, for he says 'he shot her himself.'

"Thomas W. Brown, it is true, is his brother, but it was very natural he should be about him in his imprisonment and have the opportunity to converse with Reese.

"Though Caroline Garrett was a stepdaughter, there is no presumption that her sympathies were with Brown more than Reese, for this relation often creates hostilities more than sympathy. On the contrary, her sympathies would seem to be with Reese, for he testifies that Brown offered him his daughter, which would hardly have been done without her consent, and unless Brown knew that Reese wanted her. Her intimacy with Reese, sitting on his pallet in the jail, and calling him by the caressing name of Lum, goes to show very tender feelings between them."

And what of the negroes who testified in graphic detail about what they saw and heard? Testifying in a white man's court for the first time, would they be credible? Andrews raised doubts about their motives for speaking out.

"Speaking of the credibility of witnesses, it should be remarked that though the negroes should be as intelligent and conscientious as whites, it impairs their credit when it is manifest that they would lose neither character nor self-respect by swearing falsely, a consideration which so greatly influences white witnesses. But, above all, if Brown were the cruel brute represented by the negroes, it is too much to expect of human nature that they would swear impartiality against him."

Brown now looked at Captain Western. "Sir, if it please you, Colonel Weems will advance our argument further." Western nodded his approval.

Weems stood up to address the court. As he walked around in front of his table, Andrews paused briefly and whispered to Weems before returning to his seat. Weems, who had been quiet through most of the trial, then took his turn to advance the case brought forward by the defense.

"The devices used by Brown to conceal the murder are compatible with his innocence. Besides the threat against his life by Reese, it was perfectly consistent with his innocence that he should wish to conceal it, for he knew if the body were found, he would be implicated, though he did remonstrate against the shooting. His present predicament shows that he judged rightly of the perils, trouble and expense that would follow."

Now, wagging a finger in the direction of the commission to emphasize his point, Weems slowly and precisely stated, "It was prudent to conceal it, though innocent of any participation in it."

Weems would build on the foundation laid by Andrews, that Brown at the most was a blustering bystander, certainly not a murderer.

"This case, in some of its aspects, is the most remarkable in the history of jurisprudence. That an accomplice, with a promise of mercy, should himself be put on trial, and the prisoner he accused be brought forward to convict him, is, we think, unheard of. The government has got the benefit of his evidence, and now the prosecution would cheat him by quibbles out of the mercy he is entitled to by the government."

Andrews reached across the table to hand Weems a sheet of paper containing a smattering of notes. Referring to it, Weems continued, this time focusing on Brown's confession.

"First they charge he did not make a full confession." Weems turned aside and pointed to Reese as he continued. "With the exception of Reese, there is no proof that he did not make a full one about the murder." Weems walked over to the table where Reese was sitting as he made his point. "Brown, having confessed several days before Reese, without knowing what charge, if any, would be made against him, of course he omitted to notice or explain many things brought to his attention by the witnesses since."

And Weems reminded the officers that General Wild certainly found Brown believable, as he moved back over to stand behind his chair.

"Brown had the promise of the government officer to recommend him to mercy in consideration of his turning state's evidence in this case, such as it was or might be, without any conditions." Weems paused. This time he took the paper of notes and made a sweeping motion with it. "If any such conditions were prescribed or intended, Brown in good faith should have been apprised of them, or the promise of the government will prove but a snare instead of protection."

Emphasizing each word, he went on. "This is the great end to be obtained by the promise of mercy, and in good faith, he should have it. He has made himself odious by the aid he has given the government, and turned the sympathies of the neighbors in favor of Reese, by which the latter has obtained a petition for his pardon." Weems then ripped the paper in half, tossing the pieces on the table in front of him. "This is one of the penalties he paid the government for its promise, out of which he never expected to be cheated by a lawyer's quibble.

"The prosecution says Brown has confessed no crime." Weems shrugged his shoulders, and he placed a hand on Brown's shoulder. "The promise of the government was based on no such condition....There can be no sentence pronounced against the prisoner, Brown, because there is no crime charged. If one were, it is not said to be a violation of any law, federal or state." Weems began to tap lightly on Brown's shoulder to add emphasis. "Brown is charged with only aiding and abetting Reese, without saying he aided and abetted him *willfully* and *maliciously*, though it is stated that Reese shot and killed willfully. And unless this was given willfully and maliciously, there was no crime…You cannot charge one crime and prove another."

Weems pulled his chair back and sat down. An expression of relief swept across Brown's face. He obviously felt as though Colonel Weems had acquitted himself well.

Andrews pushed his chair back to stand up to conclude the defense argument to the commission. "Apprehending he may have no other opportunity, the prisoner, John M. Brown, by his counsel, pleads and objects to any sentence, or execution of the same, founded on said charges and specification."

Andrews walked once again around to the front of his table. He reached up to adjust his black tie and pulled his coat down tight.

"First. Because there is no crime specified or set forth therein against this defendant, for which he can or should be punished."

He used his fingers to count off the points he was making.

"Second. Because it is not alleged that any crime was committed against or in violation of any law of the State of Georgia or the United States."

His eyes scanned the commission members, who were seated at a table just feet from him. Then he moved on to his final plea, recognizing that his client was probably going to be convicted, but holding out a sliver of hope that the recommendation from General Wild would carry some weight.

"But, if contrary to his expectation, sentence should be passed against this accused, he prays that the execution thereof may be placed at a day far enough distant for him to apply to proper authorities for a fulfilment of his promise of pardon."

Judge Andrews and Colonel Weems had used every legal maneuver they could muster to attack the government's case both legally and morally. Andrews returned to his seat after expending every bit of legal ammunition he had carried into the courtroom. Could this veteran country lawyer, son of a successful planter and a pious and ultra-religious Baptist mother, win over four young officers from some of the farthest reaches of the North?

Drawing from the rising whispers among the spectators on the main floor, the defense's bold case had made it clear that Brown was being railroaded to a noose. But then, the lawyers were, as they say, preaching to the choir. Not so with the negroes in the gallery. This curious thing the white people call justice was not easily understood, especially when played out by two fast-talking attorneys.

The government's advocate, young Capt. Thomas J. Rundle, was no doubt outmatched by the eloquent and thorough veteran advocates now seated at the neighboring table. But in three years of loyal service in the Union Army, Rundle had been in intense combat, watching friend and foe alike fall and never get back up. He knew what it was like to face a tough and determined opponent, and he had not survived this long for lack of instinct. It was with his own determination that he took his turn to address the commission.

Rundle, bedecked in his blue uniform, stood up from his seat and began. "The evidence in this case established that Brown is the principal in guilt. Technically, he is accessory before the fact, accessory after the fact and principal in the second degree, present aiding and abetting.

"In substance," Rundle said, briefly pausing to look down at the sheet of notes on the table in front of him, "he is much worse than even this; for while his heart was first to conceive, and his head to plan the whole matter, the malice, motive and intent were all his, and procured the motive and power and used the young man Reese as a cat's-paw, involving him in a great crime."

The white spectators began to groan, a few very loudly. They resisted the effort of the Yankee officer's slick tongue to change the way they felt about Brown. Captain Western tapped the gavel to quiet them down.

Rundle continued. "No one was present with Brown and Reese. We are dependent upon their statement for the history, and by sifting them and comparing them with known facts established by other testimony, and by their naturalness and probability, determine what is the truth of the case."

"The truth is that Brown is innocent!" a burly older man in worn blue coveralls shouted from the back of the courtroom.

"Silence!" Western shouted. "Silence. I will have the guards remove every one of you from this courtroom if there is another outburst." A guard moved over through the packed courtroom to escort the older man out, but he fled before the guard could reach him.

"Continue, Captain," Western urged.

"Brown has malicious motives and interest. In the past, Nellie's tongue had sometimes spoken out freely against his injustice. Her naked body had received many a bitter stroke, yet she was not altogether subdued. Now she is going with a report to the Yankees."

In life, Nellie never had had an advocate. No one had ever spoken up for her or defended her. But in this courtroom in Washington, Georgia, Nellie's voice was being heard loud and clear.

Rundle looked up toward the gallery, where Nellie's family members were all gathered, and spoke in their direction. "She has a story to tell, and the truth, if her own is told, is bad enough. His authority over her is gone," he said, pointing to Brown. "Her triumph is at hand. She is, or imagines she is, on her way to report him. 'Mistaken Nellie,' Brown thinks to himself, 'I have quite other plans. I will manage this matter better than that.'"

Rundle again turned to face the four commission members. "As soon as he turns to Reese, scarcely less his victim than Nellie—the middle-aged man to the stripling, the strong man to the easy and plastic youth—'It will never do,' he says, 'to let that damned bitch go to the Yankees.'"

Rundle paused. He softly repeated, "'It will never do'—a dogmatic assertion, having the weight of an agreement with a youngster." His voice began to rise louder and louder for emphasis. "It will never do—that is my verdict and deliberate opinion. She will tell on us, and there is no telling what lie she will tell, and you are as much in this scrape as I am. She is angry with you too. Remember you threatened her too this morning. Such is the talk...."

The judge advocate knew he must use Reese's confession to destroy the hot-tempered Brown as a credible source. The testimony of the victim's family members, the testimony of acquaintances, even the testimony of his own kinfolk had shined a bright light on the darkness that lives within him. It was time to drive that home to the commission.

"Brown's account of it is that Reese said he would kill her if ever he saw her again—for what? For going to the Yankees. She was not his property, nor even Brown's property. But Reese is savage on this subject. He said he had already killed two and was become knight errant to kill all who should go to the Yankees."

Rundle put the palm of his hand on his table and stiffened his arm to prop him up as he recalled the testimony. "Compare the motives of the two men and the probable truth of the narratives. They bear no comparison."

Recreating the conversation, he offered, "You are not easy to persuade into this business, Mister Reese, but I have a large offer to make. Help me out with it and I will give you anything in my power, even if it be my daughter. Reese, poor lad," he said glancing over to the young man, "wanting in strength of character, is led along to be presently pushed into crime."

Rundle again paused in his presentation. Then holding his hands up as if aiming a rifle, he broke the silence of the moment, loudly saying, "'Shoot, shoot!' cries Brown. 'Don't let her get away.' And the wretched lad shot....Dreadful deed." He lowered his hands. "No wonder that the old father of Reese should say, 'Cruel Brown, cruel Brown, to plunge my son into this crime.'

"It is painful to dwell on these things." Rundle explained, "We do not free Reese from heavy censure. But how much worse was Brown! On Sunday, probably about the time her children drove the buzzards from her body," Rundle said, again pointing to Brown, "Brown was bragging of the way he choked her. And his talk was so loud and boasting in a way as to attract the attention of the crowd generally, as well as the knot around him."

Then the prosecutor proceeded to explore the two jailhouse statements captured by General Wild.

"On Wednesday, 19th, Brown made what is strangely called his confession in which he *confesses his innocence*. He proposes to turn state's evidence, and General Wild promised to recommend him to mercy upon the usual conditions proposed, of a full and truthful narrative of the whole transaction.

"On Saturday, 22nd, Reese made his free and complete disclosure of the whole transaction. He was in substance and reality state's evidence. He confessed, not innocence, but guilt. He told the whole story. Had he been disposed to falsify, how easy to have accused Brown and excused himself. A plain and easy lie would have cleared him, and been believed."

Rundle tore further into the defense's key argument.

"A great effort is made to discredit his statement first, by showing contradictions on the different occasions. These contradictions are found mainly in mere questions of memory. The second means of impeaching Reese is by outside confessions. Private Schribner stated exactly what Reese meant, that by his confession to General Wild, he believed Brown would be cleared. This was a conclusion of law as to the effect of his confession. He supposed that if Brown did not do it with his own hands he would be cleared."

And what did that mean to Reese's credibility?

"These outside confessions of Reese to friendly jailbirds or near kin, and not used when the occasion called for them, seem to be of little weight compared with his oath, and the fact that he was implicating himself in the most thorough manner....It is incredible that he should swear falsely against Brown, and yet swear to truths to convict himself. What an inexplicable phenomenon he would be—a moral monster—upon such a suspicion."

A "moral monster?" Certainly that put it in words the spectators understood, but not necessarily agreed with, unless of course they were among those seated in the balcony. Crossing the aisle between his desk and the defense to stand close to Brown, Rundle saw that Brown was clearly unsettled by the proximity of the Yankee who now had him under attack.

"The falsity of Brown's statement is a most powerful argument against him; upon such false statements alone men have often been convicted. He had ample time to consider, and nothing but the damning character of the truth could have induced false habit. His previous character showed a fitness for the deed. The disgusting details of his cruelties toward Sam, toward Caroline, toward Nellie herself, the special object of spite, need not be dwelt upon; nor the equally disgusting attempts of his witnesses to prove that such practices were common."

And the negroes under his thumb, what of them? As Rundle explained, "...the discipline prevented them from telling their owners. They were so much of their time under Brown's control as to be afraid to tell. Old Sam explained this when he stood by and saw his wife beaten, knowing, as he said, the power Brown had over him."

Rundle reached back around to pick up a paper from his desk and hold it up toward the commission.

"This is the God's truth of the transaction, sworn to by Reese against his own life after days of anxiety and distress at night. With his old father by him when he began, the scene was an impressive one. As he approached the confession of the actual fact, the old man grew strangely pale and agitated." Rundle turned to gesture toward William Reese, seated near the front of the courtroom. "He was warned he had better leave the room. Slowly and with apparent reluctance, he began to walk, but his feet refused to carry him. Gasping for breath, he fell at full length upon the floor in swoon. When he first, after some minutes, opened his eyes, he was at once conscious of it all, and broke forth in a melancholy tone, 'My son, my son'—then turned to me and asked, 'Could I not be hung for him?'"

Rundle stepped closer to the commissioners' table. His piercing blue eyes connected with each of theirs. "This was no artificial scene. Then, with the eloquence of feeling that marked the depths of his nature, he exclaimed: 'Cruel, cruel man. My poor boy had just come back to me. How easy to persuade him into mischief, for his hands were yet red with the blood of war. He was used to scenes of carnage and bloodshed. Human life had been very cheap where he was.'"

Rundle stepped back a couple of paces to nearer his chair. "Compare his story with all the probabilities of the case. Compare it with Brown's story. The blasphemous wretch who was choking and cursing an hour before, and who the next Sunday was boastfully exhibiting the scene and showing how he did it, here melts into tears with the tearful sorrow for the 'poor old nigger,' just before the 'damned bitch.'

"He pushes Reese on, makes him the victim only in a less degree than Nellie, does his part to ruin him forever, makes him do it all, makes thorough work of it, conceals the body and starts home. Now follow the subsequent acts of guilt. He arranges to conceal as he had arranged to perpetrate."

Rundle resumed walking through the events of the day Nellie died. "What's next? He will use his cat's-paw again when the developments look ugly. He will turn state's evidence. He will travel along the edge of truth and pervert it to Reese's ruin and his own safety. And now the strong man has the weak man in the cell with him. He talks to him for some time, then Scribner is called up to hear what Reese has to say. 'He did not shoot, nor did he throw the stone. You know, Reese, that is true. Now say so.' So, Reese says it...and says Brown, 'You hear what he says.'

"In Augusta jail they are together again. Brown made him the offer of five hundred dollars—in gold, I believe it was to be—but Reese, who had told the truth on himself, with life as the forfeit, is not going to lie for Brown for five hundred dollars or other sums.

"Young Reese has pleaded guilty. He admits his crime, and prays not for justice, but for mercy. He made no terms as state's evidence. His youth and inexperience plead for him—not as themselves leading him into this crime, but as exposing him as a victim to the arts and seductions of a man both strong and cunning. Still a minor, he had been absent from home for two years or more, and there was not more eloquence than truth in the plea of his father.

"Forgive him this one great crime, and let mercy rejoice over judgment; and if the fearful expiation of blood for blood must be made, let it be extracted rather of him who conceived, proposed and urged on the shedding there of, than of the youth he used as his instrument and screen."

With those words, Rundle took his leave to return to his chair.

Captain Western and the others retired for their deliberation. The defendants in their handcuffs and shackles were returned to their cells in the county jail. And the spectators moved out onto the courthouse grounds to press their own judgments. The atmosphere was volatile to be sure. The whites remained on the grounds, while the coloreds collected themselves across the street.

Clearly, the white citizens viewed these proceedings not as a trial, but as a Northern scheme to pervert justice and railroad two of their own to the gallows. They wondered, and with good reason, did the North have no end to the cruelty and injustice it would impose on the former ruling class in the South?

As for the freedmen, they had seen and heard for themselves a negro on a witness stand in a court testifying against a white man, an overseer no less, facing a capital murder charge. They had heard vivid descriptions of the abuse in the plantation system that was to have been shed with emancipation. They had heard lawyers plead to save the lives of two white men who had killed a negro woman. Had the times really changed? They were counting on four officers from the United States Army to provide the answer.

CHAPTER 16

⸻

Wilkes County Courthouse
Washington, Georgia
October 19, 1865

THE ATMOSPHERE IN THE COURTROOM was tense. The testimony from witnesses had described the senseless and brutal murder of a crippled old negro, whose only motive was to end the abuse of freedmen on the farm of Tom West. Other witnesses sought to paint the accused, John Brown, as a man who was all bluster and would never kill anyone. And Christopher Reese? He could only hope his version of the truth would spare him the hangman's noose.

When the commission members filed into the courtroom and took their familiar seats, the conversations among the spectators quieted. Conversations about guilt and innocence, about who was right and who was wrong, about fairness and justice—all talk came to an end.

West family members filled in the gallery, taking the seats they had occupied for the past two weeks. They were not alone. Freedmen, both familiar and stranger, jockeyed to find empty spots on the benches. They all wanted to see how Yankee justice worked for the negro in the new South.

Chairman Western tapped his gavel. All became quiet.

"Captain Rundle," he started, "please read the verdict. Will the parties please stand."

At the defense tables, Brown and his lawyers and Reese and his advocate rose and faced the commissioners. No one showed any emotion. For the men who had pounded the commission members with both facts and innuendo, their sordid tale was about to come to an end.

Captain Rundle, holding a sheet of paper, began to read from it:

The commission after having maturely considered the evidence adduced, finds the accused, Christopher Columbus Reese, as follows: Of the specification, guilty; of the charge, guilty; and do there for sentence him, Christopher Columbus Reese of Taliaferro County, State of Georgia, to be hanged by the neck until he be dead, at such time and place as the commanding general may direct, all the members of the commission concurring therein.

The outcome was predictable and yet surprising. Reese appeared a bit confused. He knew he had pleaded guilty to murder but had prayed that the commission would temper their verdict with mercy. But there wasn't the slightest bit of compassion contained in the verdict he had just heard read to him.

Next, Captain Rundle read from a second sheet of paper:

The commission also find the accused, John M. Brown, as follows: Of the specification, guilty; of the charge, guilty; and do there for sentence him, John M. Brown, of the State of Georgia, to be hanged by the neck until he be dead, at such time and place as the commanding general may direct, all the members of the commission concurring therein.

For Brown the defeat was total. The commission saw through his witnesses and the legal arguments from his learned attorneys. His head fell forward, his chin resting on his chest, as he emitted a deep sigh. For perhaps the first time in his life, Brown had been held accountable for his temper and his actions.

The white spectators were furious with the outcome. Brown's wife burst into tears, Reese's parents hugged each other in disbelief, and many others rose to their feet shouting protests. Several simply left the courtroom shaking their heads. A smattering of applause was heard coming from the freedmen. Several raised arms and even a few shouted: "Yes!" "Hallelujah!" "Thank you, Jesus!" The Nellie West family had received genuine justice and reassurance that, yes, the Union army would take care of the South's colored citizens.

But not so fast. The commission wasn't quite finished. Captain Rundle had one more sheet of paper to read from. This time he turned to Reese, looking at him directly, locking eyes:

We, the undersigned, members of the military commission, charged with the trial of C. Columbus Reese and John M. Brown, citizens of the State of Georgia, charged with murder, do, in view of mitigating circumstances adduced on said trial, hereby recommend C. Columbus Reese to mercy and clemency.

This time it was Reese who released a sigh of relief. The statement left no question that the government also believed the argument that he was an impressionable young man—even at the age of 20—and was easily manipulated by the cunning Brown. But with a death sentence now hanging over his head, he would have to press his case anew in the court of public opinion, something his attorney Samuel Barnett was already doing.

A full four days before the verdict was announced, Barnett had begun collecting petitions asking for clemency, a pardon, or anything else that would spare his client from the gallows.

As early as October 16, Absolom Rhodes, John A. Taylor and A. H. Pittman had sworn before a justice of the peace that they knew Reese to be "obliging" and "easily persuaded" by an older person. And the lists of petitions signed on that same day grew rapidly with signatures of many members of the Sturtevant family, Doctor W. M Rhodes, and so many others. The next day, on the 17th, three days before sentencing, more than 100 people signed a single petition which cited among the reasons for clemency, "the excited state of public sentiment."

As the days passed, hundreds more people signed petitions on behalf of John Brown, who also was asking for a pardon from President Johnson "because of his large and helpless family, so much needing his assistance in this time of poverty and want...."

Over the following weeks, the list of signers would top 600. While justices of the peace were busy certifying the petitions, the members of the military commission packed up and left Washington.

On October 23, just four days after delivering their verdicts, Commission members Captains Western and Palmer, Judge Advocate Rundle and Provost Marshal Cooley mustered out of the army with their units in Augusta and left for the return trip to New York.

Commission members Lieutenants Baldwin and Pratt returned to their units in northeast Georgia and continued their assignment to preserve order, approve work contracts between whites and negroes, and administer the amnesty oath for another six months. Their unit was not mustered out until April 25, 1866, at Fort Pulaski, near Savannah, Georgia.

At the same time the chain-of-command review of the military commission's work was quickly moving along.

Eight days had passed since the convictions and sentencing when Brevet Maj. Gen. John H. King at military district headquarters in Augusta issued his official order:

> *The proceedings, findings and sentence in the foregoing cases of C.C. Reese and John M. Brown, citizens, are hereby approved, and respectfully forwarded for the final action of the major general commanding the department.*

Then a week later on November 4, Maj. Gen. James B. Steedman, the commander of Union troops in Georgia, completed his review. However, Steedman reserved judgment on the merits of the case:

Inasmuch as the murdered person and those committing the murder are either citizens or freedwoman, the case is respectfully forwarded to the President of the United States for action.

So, by the middle of November, just a month after the trial, the Bureau of Military Justice at the War Department in Washington was handed the murder case of Nellie West. The Judge Advocate General was the President's legal advisor in these matters and would prepare the case for review. The man who held that position, Joseph Holt, a sly Kentucky lawyer, was not one easily swayed by sentiment.

Holt had served several appointments in the Buchanan administration, including Secretary of War leading up to the Civil War. In 1862 he joined the Union Army and served as Lincoln's Judge Advocate General, a position he maintained into the Johnson Administration. Holt personally prosecuted the Lincoln assassins, insuring their execution, but was forever tainted by accusations of withholding evidence in the existence of a diary taken off John Wilkes Booth's body.

In his November 15 briefing for the President on the case involving John Brown and Christopher Reese, the veteran prosecutor stuck to the facts. Those facts included the clemency recommendation for Reese from the military commission and a "number of affidavits to the general kindness" of Reese.

The circumstances of the murder by the two prisoners of Nellie West, an aged, decrepit and crippled negro woman, harmless and without power of defense, are in the utmost degree atrocious and sickening; while the daily life and habits of the older offender, Brown, and his language and demeanor toward the unhappy creatures over whom he has been for the past five years the overseer, are such as to paralyze the imagination in its effort to picture the constant miseries and humiliation to which they must have been exposed.

Reese, Holt believed, had shown remorse in confessing the "willful and deliberate" preparation of the murder "with his own hand." His testimony concealed no part of his own responsibility "and, assuming, in atonement for his enormous guilt, his full share of the resultant responsibility to God and man, implicates Brown to the fullest extent."

> *The full confession made by Reese, whose remorse seems to be considerable… (is) amply sufficient proof of his guilty connection with the crime.…With regard to overseer Brown, who sought to shift from his own shoulders upon those of Reese the responsibility for this shocking crime… it is felt that justice demands the inexorable enforcement of the extreme penalty of the law.*
>
> *The tears, the sufferings, the soul-destroying degradation of the unhappy beings whom Providence, for some inscrutable purpose, has suffered him for years to oppress and torture, call aloud for the expiation of his many crimes upon the gallows.*

Holt left no doubt how he felt legally and morally about the fate that awaited Brown. At the same time he found no sympathy for Reese.

> *The recommendation of the court to Executive clemency in the case of Reese rests on no foundation which seems entitled to any respect. It appears to have proceeded mainly from the earnest representations of men, recently slave-holders, and who, it is quite clear from their record…look with absolute indifference, if not with full approval, upon the most revolting cruelties committed upon this hapless race of beings.*
>
> *He was twenty years of age, and was doubtless as fully conscious of the enormity of the crime he afterwards committed as if he had been thirty. Considering the sensibilities which should be inseparable from his youth, his persistence in his dastardly and bloody work shocks even more than the conduct of his hardened and ruffianly associate.*

In conclusion, Holt argued that President Johnson should affirm the decision of the military commission by saying, "If the law does not take the life of such a monster of crime as this, then it is believed that the penal code has been enacted in vain."

The President received the report on November 20.

Five days later, President Johnson responded in a way that set the stage for the January executions.

> *The foregoing proceedings, findings and sentence are approved, and it is ordered that Major General Steedman, commanding Department of Georgia, or any other officer for the time being commanding the said department, carry the said sentence into effect, by hanging the said John M. Brown and the said Christopher Columbus Reese each by the neck until he is dead, and the said place of executing the said sentence to be fixed by the commanding officer of the department, and the execution to take place on the first Friday in January next.*

The Assistant Adjutant General designated that the hangings would occur in Augusta under the supervision of Brevet Maj. Gen. John H. King, commanding the District of Augusta.

It would seem now that the matter was settled. Brown and Reese would pay for the murder of Nellie West. But some aspects of Southern justice are never settled. You see, while the case was in the course of review, events were unfolding in Crawfordville that even the President could not ignore.

Crawfordville, Georgia
October 26, 1865

THE DAY ARRIVED FOR ALEXANDER H. Stephens' return to Liberty Hall. President Johnson's early pardon had reduced Stephens' time in confinement to a mere five months. Now he was back among people who loved and adored him. People who respected him and made him the most famous—and popular—person that Crawfordville had ever produced.

"Oh, how changed are all things here! Change, change, indelibly stamped upon everything I meet, even upon the faces of the people," Stephens said on arrival at the railroad depot. "I learned at the depot that all were well at the lot and at the homestead."

The families of the freedmen of Liberty Hall gathered to greet their former master. "As we came from the depot to the house, the children— Ellen, Tim, Dora, Fanny, and Quin—all met us out by the Academy. The children all cried for joy. Dora blubbered right out. The eyes of all, except Fanny and Quin, were tearful. Eliza met us at the gate; her eyes, too, were full."

But gazing on his beloved Liberty Hall made this homecoming so sweet, exactly 24 weeks to the day after his arrest. "The house and lot looked natural and yet withal sadly changed in some respects. I seemed to myself to be in a dream. But my heart went up in fervent thanksgiving to Almighty God for preserving and guiding me back once more to this spot so dear to me."

A reporter who observed him some time after his release offered a description of the elder statesman: "Tall, excessively thin, stooped at the shoulders, with a small boyish face, bright, glittering eye, silvery hair… a soft felt hat worn negligently on the back of the head, a carelessly tied cravat under a rolling collar, and a swallow tail coat. He seemed nervous…."

Stephens returned with a yearning to be involved again in the affairs of his community and state. What better way to do that than to take up the cause of a young man facing the gallows. A heartbroken mother and a devastated father would now have someone in authority to reach out to.

No matter that Stephens was a leader of the vanquished Southern cause. He was still a man who had connections, who could get attention and who could work magic for people in his part of the world. It did not take long for Stephens to respond to the pleas of the Reese family.

He knew time was running out for the criminals; in mere weeks, Brown and Reese would hang. Their attorneys, local citizens and Stephens himself believed the moment was at hand to go back to President Johnson for another look at the case.

During the full two months since the military Commission had rendered its judgment, the citizens in Taliaferro County and beyond had done much more than just watch this case unfold. Hundreds of them actually had sought to affect the outcome.

Reese's lawyer, Samuel Barnett, had collected signatures and statements from friends and neighbors seeking mercy for his client before the trial had even ended.

Among the first recorded statements was the one from John R. Kirkland, who served in the same company with Reese during the war. "His father told me to take care of him," he wrote. "I promised to do so. I know he is very easy to influence, especially by persons older than he is…." The ally observed Reese was "easily persuaded and easily controlled, and more so than any youth I ever was acquainted with."

Two other men who served with him in the cavalry, William O. Steward and William Jones, likewise attested he was "easily influenced, especially by older people," but added they "never knew or heard of his having a difficulty with a negro before this difficulty."

People who had known Reese for years, such as M. L. Pittman, Sylvester Stewart, Dr. William Rhodes and Alexander Stewart, all described the boy as "obliging, peaceable and easily persuaded."

The prayers for mercy and clemency were contained in petitions signed by scores of citizens, all noting the "excited state of public opinion" that existed in east central Georgia.

Not be to be outdone, Andrews and Weems saw that petitions were circulated to plead for clemency for Brown, claiming his execution would leave behind a "large and helpless family, so much needing his assistance in this time of poverty and want." These petitions also contained hundreds of signatures. Each document was personally addressed to President Andrew Johnson.

As late as November 13, petitions with hundreds more signatures were still being collected on behalf of Reese, asking the President to grant a full pardon or to commute the sentence to prison time.

By mid-December, the President had even heard from Superior Court Judge William Reese of Georgia's Northern District on behalf of Reese, describing him as an "unfortunate youth." The jurist, no relation to defendant, said, "I think the cause of justice and mercy would both be subserved by the commutation of his punishment. I say this from a thorough knowledge of the facts of the case, and the feelings of this whole section of the country."

Perhaps the most shocking petition solicited was produced in early December by the most unlikely of signers—the family of Nellie West. Sixteen of the family members signed next to their printed names, each with a hand-written "X."

Justice of the Peace Graham Acree certified the "petition was signed by the petitioners of their free will and accord, without intimidation or persuasion."

It was addressed to His Excellency Andrew Johnson, President of the United States. The request was simple and direct:

We the undersigned, relatives, brother, son of Nellie West, who was killed by Columbus Reese and John Brown, would most earnestly beseech your Excellency's clemency in behalf of Columbus Reese, now confined in Augusta under sentence of death.
Ralph West (son)
Aleck West (brother)
Gabrel West (son)
Kitty West (daughter)
Lucinda West (daughter)
Sam West (brother)
William West
Milly West (sister-in-law)
Caroline West (sister-in-law)
Julia West
Willis West
Washington West
Mary West
Georgia West
Emily West
Amelia West

There was no end to the lengths that the camps of supporters for Reese and Brown would go to in order to get a favorable response from the President.

Reese's mother, Frances, would travel to Washington, D.C., to personally present the petitions on behalf of her son to President Johnson. She carried with her the endorsement of and introduction by Alexander H. Stephens, written on December 12:

This will be handed to you by Mrs. Frances A. Reese, of this county. She is the mother of Christopher C. Reese, who is under sentence of death. Her object in visiting Washington is to make an appeal to your Excellency's clemency in her son's behalf. I recommend her and her cause to your special and tender consideration. I know her, and also know her son; she is a most excellent woman, and a most devoted mother; her son is young, and without any knowledge of the facts of this case, I can but believe that he was, in what he did, under the influence of another. His youth should be some mitigation of his offense. But all the facts will be unfolded and presented by his mother, or others. The object of this is barely to say to you that the mother is a woman not only of good character; but of real worth, though moving in an humble sphere of life. Most sincerely does my heart sympathize with her in her present deep affliction.

A letter of introduction for Frances Reese to President Johnson was itself a rather simple act for Stephens to accomplish, but it was not his only involvement in this case. No, if he were to exert any influence on behalf of the family, he would have to open many more doors, including one that would get Mrs. Reese into the Executive mansion.

Back in October, on his way to Georgia from Fort Warren, Stephens had spent a few days in Washington, D.C. While there, he made the acquaintance of Sen. David Trotter Patterson of Tennessee. Patterson was President Johnson's son-in-law. The meeting would prove fortuitous for Stephens, one never reluctant to call in a favor.

He crafted a letter to Patterson on December 18 asking that Patterson assist Mrs. Reese with her efforts to see his father-in-law while she was in Washington. The letter read as follows:

I presume upon the slight acquaintance I formed with you in my passage through Washington, and your well known character, to give a letter to Mrs. Reese of this county to you. Her visit to Washington is on a case of life or death for her son; her name is Frances A. Reese, and she is the mother of Christopher C. Reese, now in Augusta jail in this State under sentence of death. The execution is ordered to take place on the first Friday in January. She has but a few days to act in; she goes to

Washington to make an appeal to the President's mercy. If a pardon cannot be granted, she asks a commutation of the sentence to imprisonment for life, if no shorter time can be granted. She has numerous petitions; one from quite a number of the near relatives of the woman he killed. This petition I thought would be worth all the best; it shows the feelings of those most interested in the deceased. Mr. Acree, the justice of the peace before whom this petition was signed, is well known to me, and full faith may be given to his certificates. I had heard of the sympathy manifested by the relatives of the unfortunate who was shot, and by all means that their petition should be got. I know Mrs. Reece well, and deeply sympathize with her in her deep affliction. May I ask you to aid her in getting an early interview with the President and to call his special attention to the petition of the relatives of the deceased? I do think that ought, and will perhaps have weight with him.

Having made his case for the meeting, Stephens added one more thought:

P.S. – Mrs. Reese is a very poor woman, and deserves the sympathy of all.

—◆—

CHAPTER 18

Common Jail
Augusta, Georgia
December 1865

BY THE WINTER OF 1865, the City of Augusta once again had regained the prominence it had enjoyed during and prior to the war. The ravages of combat were not visited on this place, which had offered a brisk business manufacturing arms, ammunition, clothing and flour around the clock to support the Southern cause. Among the survivors of the war were 10 warehouses capable of holding 100,000 bales of cotton.

The city's 10,000 residents still harbored ill feelings from the war, feelings that were more deeply imbedded than in other parts of the state. The people were described as generally anxious and dejected, and fearful—fearful of harsh measures from the occupying Yankees. But more so than their fellow countrymen in other parts of Georgia, Augusta's white population seemed more willing to acquiesce to the current conditions.

While serving as the center of commerce for the region, Augusta was also the headquarters for the federal occupation army in Georgia. Hundreds of Union soldiers made camp in the city as they administered martial law.

Preparations were being made at the former Confederate Powder Works to ready the gallows for the two killers from Raytown. The fate of

Christopher Reese and John Brown was sealed. Their deaths were inevitable and just weeks away.

Petitions had been collected—petitions signed by hundreds of family, friends and strangers, including the victim's own family. Reese's mother engaged in a personal mission to meet with President Johnson to plead for mercy. Alec Stephens was working, too, in direct and personal ways to reverse the course of military justice. Clearly, the passing of time allowed for a headwind to build against the actions taken by the military commission.

Then, in the middle of December, something unexpected happened. With much haste Augusta banker Joseph P. Carr dispatched an important new document to the President in Washington, D.C. The communication was urgent and needed the executive's immediate attention. Time was running out.

This was not a matter to be easily dismissed because Carr had retrieved from the Augusta jail something that he believed on its own face would change the course of justice. He had in his hands a new confession from Christopher Reese.

He cast his pleadings to Johnson this way:

> *The humble petition of the undersigned, a citizen of Augusta, in the State of Georgia, respectfully showeth that John M. Brown and Christopher C. Reese are now confined in the jail at this place, under sentence of death, for the murder of one Nellie West, a freedwoman; that the said Reese has made the enclosed confession, which seems to exonerate the said Brown, and to offer some mitigating circumstances in his own behalf. Your petitioner, therefore, prays such action in the premises as to you may seem meet, and will ever pray.*

Reese's new statement "exonerated" the man who drove him to kill the woman. His new statement offered "mitigating circumstances." Just what drama had played out behind the scenes in the Augusta jail? Remember that Brown at one time had announced in the jail an offer of up to $500 to Reese if he would take the fall. Had Reese taken the bait? Had the government's star witness at trial not been truthful?

This new version of events was taken down by 1ˢᵗ Lt. William Krause of the 19ᵗʰ U.S. Infantry, the commander of the jail. It was witnessed by 1st Lt. James H. Patterson of the same unit:

> *Before me, the undersigned authority, personally appeared Christopher Columbus Reese, who, being duly sworn, makes oath and says: That being under sentence of death by the judgment of a military commission held at Washington, Georgia, about the first day of October A. D. 1865, and that said sentence having been approved by the President of the United States, and on the first Friday in January 1866, set for the day of execution; and having the fear of death before his eyes, and desiring to do justice so far as he is able to all men, and particularly to John M. Brown, who was tried and convicted at the same time and on the same charge, and sentenced to execution at the same time, and as this deponent believes upon his statement, made before the commission, there being no witnesses of the murder of Nellie West, the colored woman, of which they were convicted, but themselves, this deponent saith, upon his oath, and as he expects to appear soon before his judgment-seat of Almighty God, that the following is the true statement of the facts in the case:*
>
> *That on or about the 13ᵗʰ day of July, A. D. 1865, having stayed at the house of the said John M. Brown on the previous night, this deponent and the said Brown went out hunting directly after breakfast. They went across the railroad toward Mr. Moor's plantation, and in a thicket or strip of timbered land, near Moore's, met the woman Nellie West. Brown, having stopped in the bushes to attend to a call of nature, was about fifty yards off when this deponent met the said woman. This deponent asked her if she were the woman for whom he had written a note that morning to Captain Cooley, provost marshal at Washington. She answered, "What is it to you, you some of a bitch?"*

Deponent discovered then that she had in her hand a piece of scythe blade, and about one foot and a half long. She commenced to calling Willis and Ralph, two other negroes, and made at deponent with the knife and scythe blade. Deponent asked what she meant. She said she was going to kill him; this deponent retreating as she advanced. This deponent then fired his gun—a small squirrel rifle—and struck her, as he afterwards found, in the abdomen. She fell on her hands and knees, and this deponent picked up a rock and throwing it struck her in the head. She then fell.

When she called for the negroes Willis and Ralph, the said Brown came running up, but this deponent shot just before Brown reached him. Brown asked if the deponent had hit her. Deponent said he did not know. Both went up to where she lay, about ten steps off, and Brown asked what she was doing with the scythe blade. Deponent said she had tried to kill him, and asked if Brown had seen her advancing on him. Brown replied he did, and heard her call the negroes.

This deponent then picked up the scythe blade and threw it away. Brown and deponent then returned to Brown's house. On the way Brown told deponent that the negroes had threatened his (deponent's) life on account of some watermelons; and that one of them had tried to borrow his (Brown's) gun for that purpose.

This deponent further states that he made this statement to his attorney Samuel Barnett, Esq., and to W. J. Reese, his father, and they advised deponent to implicate Brown as a means of saving his (deponent's) life; to say that Brown had offered deponent his step-daughter, Caroline Garrett, in marriage if he would kill said Nellie West; and after the murder, that he offered deponent five hundred dollars to say that he (Brown) had nothing to do with it.

And they counselled him to declare that Brown handed deponent the rock to throw at said Nellie; whereas the truth was, that Brown had not yet come up to deponent when he threw the rock at her. But this deponent yielded to their advice, and swore falsely against the said Brown in the above particulars and in many others of slight consequence.

> *And he now makes this affidavit freely and voluntarily, without any*
> *influence of said Brown and only in the hope of securing his justice.*
> *The only person who has spoken to deponent on the subject is one of*
> *the guards, a soldier named Schribner, who advised him to make a full*
> *confession, but does not know, even now, what this deponent would say.*
>
> *And further this deponent saith not, remembering at this time noth-*
> *ing more that is material.*

The name C.C. Reese was signed at the bottom, and the two union officers attested to what Reese had just told them:

> *We, the undersigned, were both present at the preceding confession, and*
> *certify that the said C.C. Reese made the same freely and voluntarily, and*
> *so declared in our presence and to us.*

Indeed, this new version of events was explosive. It had the potential to
blow up this case in the worst place, at the worst time. It was a distraction
President Johnson did not need. He was in the process of frying bigger
fish, preoccupied with consequences of unsettled race relations across
the South, as he shared in a message to the Senate:

> *Perplexing questions were naturally to be expected from the great and sudden*
> *change in relations between the two races, but systems are gradually develop-*
> *ing themselves under which the freedmen will receive the protection to which*
> *he is justly entitled, and, by means of his labor, make himself a useful and*
> *independent member of the community in which he had his home.*

If the federal government were going to be the source of protection for
the negro and provide that protection with any credibility, cases like Nellie
West's murder should not be the subject of second-guessing. Justice should
be dispensed fairly and impartially. However, the case had become infected
by Southern politics, and Johnson would have to take sides.

The confession arrived on the desk of Judge Advocate General Holt, who had already advised the President to sustain the decision of the military commission. Without reservation, Johnson initially signed off on the executions. Now confronted with their star witness' new confession and with the date of the executions rapidly approaching, Holt had a hard time containing his emotions as he once again advised the President in a memorandum on December 23:

The enclosed paper, purporting to be an affidavit made by C.C. Reese, now under sentence of death for murder, before 1ˢᵗ Lieutenant Krause, 19ᵗʰ United States Infantry, commanding jail in Richmond County, is to the effect that J. M. Brown, also sentenced to be hung on the same day for participation in the same crime, is wholly innocent, and that the affiant committed the homicide in self-defense.

The opinion of this bureau touching the mutual and unquestionable guilt of the two persons, Brown and Reese, which led it to recommend most earnestly to the Executive that the death sentence should be carried out, remains wholly unaltered by this document. It is manifestly not only replete with falsehoods, though purporting to be made with the fear of death before the affiant's eyes, but is the result of most infamous influence brought to bear upon the wretched young man by friends and in behalf of his even more guilty associate, Brown....

...The motive of the enclosed affidavit is patent. Its design clearly is to obtain, firstly, the release and pardon of one of the assassins, and subsequently to make use of the expected credulity of the government, and its reliance on a paper prepared under circumstances of solemnity, to accomplish the release and pardon of the other.

The evidence of Reese's participation in the alleged and proven murder was in part his own confession at trial. (In) every single statement... he is corroborated in the fullest and most conclusive manner.

Brown also confessed his presence at the scene of crime.... Every action on Brown's part demonstrate(s) his guilt. His education as an overseer on a plantation is proof of his fitness for the crime he afterwards committed. He is shown to have made for years the planta-tion he governed a very hell upon earth for his hapless workmen. He is shown to have manifested the most barbarous ferocity in the inflic-tion of punishment....One of his own witnesses testifies that he was a 'very wicked man'.... His acknowledged presence at the murder, and his secrecy and numerous falsehoods subsequent to it, are sufficient in themselves to justify the findings of the court.

The affidavit now submitted, the effect of which is to acquit both the prisoners, is in many respects a remarkable document. It alleges that Nellie, on discovering Brown and his confederate near her, called out loudly for Willie and Ralph (who were both at work in a distant field, out of sight and far away) and rushed at Reese with a broken scythe, avow-ing her intention to kill him. What necessity existed, even under these circumstances, for taking her wretched life?

All the evidence shows that she was not only aged and feeble, but lame in the knee and maimed in one of her feet, the big toe of which was nearly cut off. Could not Reese alone, still more with Brown to aid him, have easily disarmed her? Was it not in his power by walk-ing away...to have kept her out of reach? ...Up to the present moment have neither uttered a syllable about self-defense, a broken scythe, or calls for Willis and Ralph.

The statement is palpably an afterthought, suggested by Brown's friends to Reese as a loop-hole for his own escape from the just vengeance of the law to induce him to swear to a falsehood almost on his dying day....

Finally, and to cap the climax of his wickedness, he swears in the affidavit that he perjured himself at his trial by the advice of his own father and counsel.... What a charge to bring false and infamous as it is proved to be, against a father, whose misery at his son's crime was such that he fainted and fell to the floor insensible at the first examination of the criminals, and on returning to life openly accused Brown of the ruin of his boy.

The attention of the President is respectfully called to the signifi-cant fact that not a particle of proof is given with this affidavit of

Reese's to lend probability to his shocking charge. The whole statement is one issue of falsehoods from the beginning to end....The opinion is again expressed that no reliance is to be placed in this affidavit attesting to the innocence of both, and that it furnishes, if possible, additional proof of the necessity of enforcing to its full extent the sentence pronounced by the court.

Holt's memo would not be the last word. As he had faithfully done time and again for President Lincoln, Holt regularly advised Johnson on military pardons. The two were known to spend hours considering the pleas for intervention by the executive. Holt would summarize the charges and offer his own opinion on the evidence, the sentence and any input from others who may have reviewed the cases. The President was the one who often looked for ways to justify commutations. Holt on the other hand would take a much harder line.

Such was the case on December 27, 1865, with the execution now just days away. The General Order directing the hangings had been issued by the Department of Georgia just five days earlier. And for one final time Holt would urge the President to hold firm.

"General Holt, I cannot imagine that the killing of a colored woman would be the subject of so much attention," President Johnson lamented. "And Stephens' intervention is not making this any easier sending a distraught mother up here with countless petitions for favor."

Tired and frustrated, Andrew Johnson continued suffering his baptism by fire. Just eight months earlier he had been plucked from the governor's mansion in Tennessee to be Abraham Lincoln's Vice President. Then destiny had dealt Johnson another hand with the assassination of Lincoln in April and the end of fighting between the North and South.

"Mister President, until civil order is restored in the South, our use of military commissions to adjudicate grievances and crimes will only compound our work, I fear," General Holt replied. "Even a murder case like this one—cut and dry, I would say—depends on your final disposition, which you have already given."

But not even the final determination by the President of the United States himself could withstand the hurricane-force winds of Southern politics. An appeal was back at the White House for yet one more look.

Sitting behind his desk cluttered with papers and reports, Johnson was quick to dig into the matter at hand, giving no hint of what he was thinking. His expression was a mix of sadness and earnestness.

"General Holt…why is this case back before me on this day?"

"Sir," Holt began as he lifted a stack of papers from the corner of the desk. "This, Mister President, is why we are here again." He held the papers out with extended hands, mildly shaking them. "These are letters and petitions with over six hundred signatures asking for you to pardon these two killers!

"This is simply outrageous!" Holt exclaimed, as he firmly placed the papers back onto the desk and took a seat opposite the President.

Johnson sat patiently, waiting to hear his legal advisor's renewed argument.

"If I may, sir?" Holt inquired, running a hand through his ample head of graying hair.

Johnson leaned back in his plush leather chair. "Yes, please continue. Somehow I sense you are not satisfied with the course this case has taken."

"Not satisfied? That's not the half of it," the Democrat-turned-Radical Republican replied. Clearly his anger was beginning to show. "Alec Stephens and his cohorts have left telltale signs all over this case! And you, Mister President, should not fall for their deception. Why these letters—they're nearly identical language—and the signatures—obviously signed by the same hand."

"I don't know that I find that so unusual, General Holt," Johnson said, interrupting. "As long as the people gave their permission to be included, why discount them?"

"With all due respect, sir, how are we to know that is indeed the case? None of these signers present facts or arguments that are not already before you.

"For example, Stephens asks for clemency for Reese based on his 'youth and inexperience.'" Holt leaned toward Johnson to emphasize his point. "Youth? Ha! Reese is twenty years old. And inexperience? The boy fought with the Confederate cavalry!"

Holt paused for a moment as he thumbed through the letters and petitions, finding just the one he was searching for. Johnson looked on through his piercing eyes, rarely smiling.

"And most grievous of all is this letter with the names of sixteen of the freedwoman's relatives very clearly printed out. Each followed by an "X" denoting their signatures. All attested to by a justice of the peace that Stephens personally vouches for. And the letter..."

"Yes, Mister Holt?" inquired the President, again interrupting.

"And the letter from these family members is a petition for clemency!" Holt leaned toward the center of the desk, while lowering his voice.

His body abruptly shot back upright. "Mister President, no doubt there is a lot of questionable justice being handed out by our military commissions and the Freedmen's Bureau, but let there be no mistake about this case."

Holt rose from his chair. "Your Bureau of Military Justice has reviewed this matter most judiciously and remains convinced that justice is best served with the execution of these two men."

Johnson responded, "And you personally agree?"

"Without a doubt! The barbarity of this murder, committed by Reese with his own hand. The cruel and unprovoked threats of death to this aged, feeble and despairing woman. And his perjury in the presence of the Almighty. These are all arguments that aggravate the original crime and justly take from Reese every ground on which he could base a hope of executive favor."

"You do not agree with Alec that this is the result of 'youth and inexperience'?" the President asked.

"Not by any definition." Holt was becoming more emotional as he continued his argument. "Reese's attempt to deceive the government into a belief of Brown's innocence by an affidavit sworn to by him when on the threshold of death, replete with falsehoods from beginning to end, has already been exposed."

By this time Holt was pacing back and forth in front of the desk. "That sons, daughters and other relatives of the defenseless victim should have voluntarily and without solicitation or threat, joined in these groundless prayers for a pardon for their mother's murderer is wholly unnatural and incredible."

The President sat up in his chair and leaned toward Holt. "You have no doubt as to what decision I should render?"

Holt sat back down to conclude his argument. "No sir. I recommend in the strongest terms that these incredulous petitions be disregarded and that Reese and Brown be suffered by your order to atone with their lives for the life of the poor, crushed woman, whom they so deliberately slew without cause."

Johnson stood up and stepped away from his chair. "So...this is my reward for giving Alec his early parole...."

CHAPTER 19

Augusta, Georgia
December 1865

IT HAD BEEN A WEEK since Frances Reese had made her pilgrimage to see the President. She had passed the time both wondering and worrying. Winter on a farm was a sequence of gray, chilly days and dark, cold nights. The uncertainty whether her son would be spared an early death had consumed her thoughts and spirit.

One day had passed without a response. Then another day. And then another.

As time advanced toward the date with the executioner, the prisoners had begun anticipating the short wagon ride across town to the gallows at the former Confederate Powder Works down on the city canal.

A large crowd would generally gather for such an occasion, but only those people with permits issued by the Provost Marshal could get onto the grounds to witness the administration of justice. The gallows had been constructed for maximum viewing—and maximum effect. The platform, at 12 feet above the ground, left plenty of room below its trap door for a man in a lone instant to feel the jerk of the noose around his neck, and for his lifeless body to flail and swing on the rope extending from the crossbeam above.

Brown and Reese were well aware of the Union Army's commitment to hang prisoners—the Lincoln assassins and the former commander of the Confederate prison at Andersonville among them. The gallows made no distinction between people who were well-connected and those who were not. Neither white nor negro. Neither man nor woman. Neither military nor civilian.

During their five months as prisoners in the Augusta jail, the celebrated killers from Raytown had come to know their cellmates—an odd mix of company from petty thieves to cold-blooded killers. Among them was Isaac, a freedman ordered by a military commission to hang for killing his former master about the same time Nellie West was murdered. Isaac, too, was protesting his innocence, but who was a negro to turn to in order to be saved from the noose? Surely not the President of the United States. A visiting preacher could offer Isaac only the consolation of religion.

Among the cellmates was also a well-heeled young Augusta man, Frank Hight, and his two associates. Their vicious murder of a Freedmen's Bureau agent shocked the entire community. Oddly, at a time when white citizens were furious about what they considered the Bureau's overreach in their lives, this murder had nothing to do with that work. No, the government agent had become embroiled in a lover's triangle. And the object of his affections? Why a negro woman, no less.

It is a tale worth retelling.

Capt. Alexander Heasley was a handsome young specimen of manhood. Tall and lean, he was a man whose flowing dark hair and sharp features would have caught the attention of any woman on either side of the Mason-Dixon Line. Just barely in his mid-20's, he brought his company of negro soldiers from the 33rd U.S. Colored Troops to Augusta to administer post-war martial law.

Four years of chasing Rebels along the Carolina coast and through Florida, much of it living with and fighting alongside colored soldiers, surely influenced Heasley's views of negroes. He had observed that they "get awfully excited at times." He wrote that he enjoyed their singing and dancing. "It is as good as theater," he said, "and the house is crowded full every time they preach."

He felt rather comfortable and at home with the coloreds, so it came as no surprise that when time came to muster out of the army and head back to his native Pennsylvania, Heasley decided instead to stay in Augusta. By late summer he was mixing among the locals while working as an agent of the Freedmen's Bureau. Heasley now had the power of the U.S. government to solve the negroes' problems and to resolve the complicated issues of their freedom and relations with white people.

But Heasley did not make his choice to stay in the South based on any great sense of duty. No, he found a more personal reason. Within weeks of his posting in Augusta, Heasley had met Sarah Jane Blakely, a very attractive mulatto woman whose Broad Street home offered him comfort during the day and consolation at night. Alex and Sarah Jane quickly made plans to marry. A match made in heaven perhaps, but one that did not sit well with three white Augusta men.

You might naturally think the whites would deride Heasley simply for his love of a negro, a taboo mixing of the races. Whites might curse the Yankee officer, call him a "nigger-lover," threaten him with lynching, or, at the very least, a tar and feathering; however, conduct similar to Heasley's by Southern gentlemen goes unchallenged as a part of their culture. Otherwise, how would one account for the many mixed-race children on plantations? No, in this case, there was another man involved. The woman of rounded features and olive skin was also the girlfriend of one of the three angry white Augusta men, specifically Frank Hight.

This is not a tale about race. It is a story about fatal attraction. Short and wiry with a scruffy beard, Hight was determined to send the Northerner packing. He carefully planned a confrontation with the Yankee who had captured the heart of his paramour.

Hight had adopted Augusta as home just like Heasley had. Coincidentally, like Heasley, Hight was from Pennsylvania. However, he had shed his Yankee roots and gone to war in 1861 with Ramsey's First Georgia Volunteers. Within a year he was back in Augusta and joined the city fire department. His fire company organized into the Georgia

Light Guards and went on to serve with the Army of Northern Virginia. But in 1863 an unspecified disability sent Hight back home, where he next found work on the railroad.

Hight needed help to carry out his scheme against Heasley and found a pair of willing recruits in two of his army buddies, Josh Doughty and Charlie Watkins. Doughty, the son of a prominent cotton merchant, dropped out of Richmond Academy in 1861 to fight in the war. A tough guy with a husky build, he was twice wounded, then captured and later sent home in a prisoner of war exchange. Watkins, tall and slim with a quiet demeanor, was a clerk in a Broad Street dry goods store when the war broke out. He served in the later years of fighting in Cobb's Legion cavalry, which toughened him up quite a bit and nurtured his hate of the North.

So on the hot, steamy night of August 30, Hight, Doughty and Watkins, three combat-tested friends, each armed with a pistol and Bowie-knife, slipped into the darkness of Augusta's back streets on their final mission. Around midnight they unexpectedly appeared at the front door of Sarah Jane's house. There they found the captain in the arms of Hight's woman. The encounter did not end well.

Watkins was anxious to dispatch the former blue coat immediately but hesitated. This delay offered Heasley a brief opportunity to try to drive the intruders from the house. Instead, three bullets fired by Watkins and Hight dropped Heasley to the floor. The sound from the shots was deafening. Through the fog of grey smoke, Watkins was seen ensuring the deed was finished by plunging his knife three times into Heasley's body, now bloodied and writhing in pain.

Sarah Jane screamed uncontrollably as the men quickly fled the house. It didn't take long for the federal authorities to round them up. General Steedman was furious that a government agent had been so brutally murdered. He was determined to see the perpetrators all hang. A military tribunal was convened at Augusta City Hall within days of the killing; however, it would take a full two months and several twists and turns to get to a verdict.

Steedman appointed as president of the commission the no-nonsense Lt. Col. Homer B. Sprague of the 13th Connecticut Volunteers, who had been cited for his "gallant and meritorious service" in the siege at Port Hudson. Also on the panel were Lt. Col. Alfred Neafle of the 156th New York Volunteers; from the 19th U.S. Infantry, Capt. George S. Pierce, who once chaired a military commission that ordered a soldier shot for desertion; and Capts. A. H. Andrews and E. P. Evans. Prosecuting the case would be a veteran of the skirmishing around Chattanooga, Judge Advocate Capt. E. L. Smith of the 19th U.S. Infantry.

Hight and his cohorts, the products of Augusta's most well-known families, did not lack for representation. Their team of barristers included Col. Joseph B. Cumming, who was described as an "orator of forcefulness and rare charm"; Judge William T. Gould, a Connecticut native who had established a law school in Augusta; and the superintendent of the city schools, A. H. McClaws. Four other attorneys assisted them.

Standing before the panel of military officers, the three shackled men, all looking pale, worn and tired, protested their innocence. It did not help them that a bloody knife had been found under Watkins' bed pillow the night he was arrested, and the empty worn leather sheath was hanging from his belt.

The strongest evidence was the eyewitness testimony from the object of the men's competing affections, Sarah Jane Blakely. She had seen it all—the confrontation, the shooting, the stabbing. But would the commission see it as she had witnessed it? Would it be enough to cause these three men to hang for the murder of Alex Heasley?

The trial began on an unusually warm early September morning. The stifling council room and adjacent halls were filled with friends and acquaintances—all waiting for the outcome. The murder was the biggest thing to hit the city since the arrival in April of Gen. Emory Upton to receive the surrender of the Augusta Arsenal. Even the man who convened the commission, General Steedman, sat in on the proceedings from time to time, despite having received a number of death threats from anonymous writers.

The defense knew it would have a tough fight for an acquittal. Judge Gould began by objecting to the right of a military commission to try the men, since they were civilians and not in any way subject to military control. This was similar to the argument that would be advanced in the trial of Reese and Brown in their failed attempt to halt their proceedings the following month. Colonel Cumming argued that military law could not, of right, be made applicable to the case because no rebellion against the United States existed in Georgia. He went on to point out the provisional governor had ordered the civil magistrates to exercise their lawful powers that were in force prior to secession—powers which included trying civilians.

For the government Gen. C. H. Grosvenor, the Provost Marshal General for the Department of Georgia, defended the lawfulness of the trial because the state was under martial law. The commission agreed with the general. The commission also ruled the three men would be tried together.

The trial got off to a fitful start. Maj. James W. Stinchcomb recounted the arrest of the suspects in the dead of night within a couple hours of the killing. The 43-year-old infantry officer described the large Bowie-knife he had found under Watkins' pillow. It wasn't until after sunrise that he examined it for blood stains, which he observed on one side. Oddly, the ever-efficient Ohioan did not bring the knife to court for the officers to examine for themselves, so he was dispatched to return with it.

That may have been the first hiccup, but it wasn't the last. One of the soldiers guarding Sara Jane in the home where the murder had occurred made a startling announcement. Sgt. Bryce Hays informed the commission that he had been approached by one of the defense attorneys, who offered him wine and money for assistance in accessing the prosecution's star witness. That may have been the way things were done in the South, but the Yankee court would have no part of such conduct. The commission president, Colonel Sprague, responded by kicking the lawyer out of the courtroom for the duration of the trial.

Dozens of prosecution witnesses, many of them negroes, passed through the witness chair in the days that followed. The heat in the chambers was described as intense, but spectators continued to show up, especially young men of the city—the prisoners' contemporaries.

One of the more odd moments of the proceeding came when Captain Smith, the Judge Advocate, stated that one of his more important witnesses, Doctor Boucher, had sent a note saying he could not attend to court at the appointed time because of illness. After some deliberation, the court, prisoners and attorneys all went to the physician's room on Broad Street to take down his testimony. Once satisfied that they had gotten what they came for, the court reconvened at city hall.

The trial testimony took only a matter of days, but the deliberations dragged on for months. By the time General Steedman got the verdict in November and reviewed the proceedings, finding and sentence, no one would hang. The path to justice was as tangled as a Georgia briar patch.

Doughty was acquitted outright. Yes, he had been along with the others with the intent of killing Heasley, but in the end he did not fire his gun or stab the victim. Culpability did not equate to responsibility in the eyes of this court.

On the other hand, Watkins, who had taken the most active role in the murder, provided the most conflicting moments for the commission. His crimson-coated knife notwithstanding, the officers simply could not agree whether he was guilty of murder. Without a unanimous finding, Watkins would not hang. He would owe his freedom less to Yankee justice than to Watkins' fiancée. You see, later it was found that the two members of the commission who favored acquittal were boarding at that young woman's house and were subjected to numerous retreatments concerning Watkins' innocence.

As for the man who hatched the plot to murder the federal agent, there was no doubt. A man had died, and someone had to be held accountable. Frank Hight was the chief actor in the scheme—he went to Sarah Jane's house with the intent to kill Heasley and indeed had shot him. Hight was the only one of the three prisoners the commission convicted. And they sentenced him to hang for the killing.

As the reviewing official, General Steedman faced a dilemma. Three men participated in a murder, but only one was being held accountable. Even though he wanted all three to hang, the general could not square the verdicts with Hight's death sentence. Steedman was compelled to administer his own justice. His choice was to allow Hight to escape the gallows and instead serve 15 years in the infamous prison in Auburn, New York.

The verdicts put Doughty and Watkins back on the street, while Frank Hight would remain locked up in the Augusta jail into December, awaiting his transfer up north. Friends and family came to visit, except for his father, who died during the trial, leaving Hight's mother a widow.

Even though this was a Yankee court, the murder case was subject to Southern justice, where things, as we have learned, are not as they seem. So it would be for Frank Hight. Being spared the gallows in exchange for 15 years in a Northern prison would not do for Hight. He still had another card to play.

President Andrew Johnson, you recall, was the final word on military commission proceedings. It didn't take long for Hight's friends to collect petitions asking the Executive for clemency, claiming the prisoner was the sole support of a now-widowed mother.

Time passed quickly. Hight left the city in early December for prison, while his companions, Watkins and Doughty, had long since been turned back onto the streets.

Hight's new home, the prison at Auburn, was the focus of a new experiment in incarceration. Corporal punishment of inmates was no longer an acceptable practice. The rods and whips previously used to administer beatings had been tucked away. The new way to handle the prisoners was with silence; inmates were simply not allowed to speak with each other. This would be Frank Hight's world for the next 15 years. Or would it?

The arm of Southern justice has a long reach, even into the quiet confines of a prison as far away as New York. President Johnson reviewed the case—and the petitions. Perhaps it was his concern for a widowed mother or his disdain for military commissions trying civilians that led him to his conclusion. In either case, the President found enough room to pardon Hight, and he would be back in Augusta within six months.

John Brown and Christopher Reese had gotten to know all three men very well during their extended stay in the city jail. They were cellmates with a common bond and on similar courses through the system of military justice. They all came from families with friends in high places. They all hoped for the same favorable outcome.

What of Isaac, the negro who killed his white overseer—the colored lad who shared the same city jail cell with the more privileged white killers. No one of power stepped forward on Isaac's behalf. No one of consequence was there to save his pitiful life from the hangman's noose that awaited him at the Powder Works.

Reese and Brown had to believe that lives of the two white men from Raytown were more valuable—much more valuable—than that of a colored man or woman. Why else would Stephens, who personally believed coloreds were not equal to whites, advocate on their behalf?

As the men waited in jail, the people in Taliaferro County had done everything they knew to do to make sure President Johnson did not ignore Christopher Reese and John Brown.

———◆———

Liberty Hall
Crawfordville, Georgia
January 2, 1866
Just three days before the scheduled execution, a telegram arrived at Liberty Hall. Alexander Stephens knew immediately it was important by the name of the sender, Brevet Maj. Gen. John H. King, commanding the District of Augusta. Mail from the Union commander was not part of the routine communications at Stephens' home.

Stephens fumbled with the paper as he unfolded the missive. A second folded piece of paper fell out onto the floor. The handwritten message he was holding read in part, "Please find enclosed a copy of orders suspending the execution of the sentence of the military commission."

Stephens let out one huge sigh as his hand holding the paper dropped to his side. Not only had he prevailed on behalf of the Reese family, but also he had validated to himself that he was still a political force to be reckoned with not just in Georgia, but far beyond. Indeed. Had there ever been any doubt?

But was it true? Was the execution really not going to happen, or was this communication possibly one big mistake?

He reached down to pick up the paper that had fallen onto the floor. As he opened it, he could see the return address: "The Executive Mansion, Washington, D.C." He knew right away who had sent it. Stephens began reading, "The execution of the sentence of the military commission in the cases of John M. Brown and Christopher C. Reese to be hung on the first Friday in January is hereby suspended until further orders. Acknowledge the receipt of this telegram." On the signature line was the name Andrew Johnson. This was a copy of the telegram Andrew Johnson had sent directly to General King.

It was not by happenstance that Stephens had received notification of the presidential order. In his confirmation telegram back to the President, Brevet Maj. Gen. John Milton Brannan, who just weeks earlier had assumed command of the Department of Georgia, reported: "Copy furnished Hon. A. H. Stephens for his information."

Actually, President Johnson had signed the stay of execution the same day his judge advocate general made that final plea to allow the decision of the military commission to stand. It took seven days for the order to reach Augusta—just 72 hours short of the scheduled execution.

What was the reasoning Johnson used to postpone the executions of Reese and Brown? Was it the "youth and inexperience" of Reese, as Stephens had pointed out? Was it the military commission's recommendation for leniency in Reese's case? Was it General Wild's recommendation for mercy for Brown? Was it the petition signed by members of Nellie West's family? Was it the direct plea from Reese's mother? Maybe it was the second confession from Reese?

Or was it the personal intervention of "Little Alec"?

Perhaps a kernel of the President's reasoning was contained in his veto of the Freedmen's Bureau bill on February 19, 1866. Congress had passed the bill over the objection of Johnson, who was inclined to return to the states of the South control of their own affairs as soon as possible. On the other hand, Congress had used the legislation to express its will that the federal government should manage Reconstruction with a firm, and some say, a punitive hand.

Johnson feared the bill was an extension of permanent military control over the South. He believed Military Commissions would continue to dispense judgment "without intervention of a jury, and without any fixed rules of law or evidence." Trials would proceed on the basis of charges and specifications, not indictments from grand juries. And Johnson argued that from the "arbitrary tribunals there lies no appeal, no writ of error." He lectured Congress on that point:

> *I cannot reconcile a system of military jurisdiction of this kind with the words of the Constitution, which declares that 'no person shall be held to answer for a capital or otherwise infamous crime unless by a presentment or indictment of a grand jury'...and that 'in all criminal prosecutions the accused shall enjoy the right to a speedy and public trial by an impartial jury of the State or district wherein the crime shall have been committed.'*

Without question the West murder case fell within the parameters of his thinking. Whether Johnson felt that specific case cried out for correction by executive nullification or whether good old Southern politics between the former Tennessee governor and the former Confederate Vice President prevailed may never be known.

What is known is that Reese and Brown never hanged for the West murder, nor did anyone else. Neither did they warm a bed in a federal prison. The two were back in Raytown to begin the new year, blessed with their own newfound freedom, courtesy of President Andrew Johnson.

———•———

Liberty Hall
Crawfordville, Georgia
March 27, 1883

Josiah had done an excellent job, I thought, in laying out the nuances of this murder case. So thorough, in fact, that I returned my notepad to my coat pocket.

"In any other circumstance, this would be the end of the story." Josiah began. "These events themselves are sufficient to provoke discussion for generations to come, as I am sure your newspaper article will do."

I nodded in agreement.

"But you would be wrong to believe this is the conclusion because there is more. Much more to tell about a young farmer, his esteemed patron, a judge and a governor."

I pulled my notepad back out of my pocket.

CHAPTER 20

---◆---

Washington, Georgia
Late 1865-Early 1866

THE TRIAL OF THE WEST killers was just a minor piece of the much larger puzzle of rebuilding lives and society under Reconstruction. Sam Barnett, Colonel Weems and the Union soldiers all moved on, as did the defendants, West and Brown. But for two of the important players in this drama, their personal fortunes were far from settled with the conclusion of the case.

Defense attorney Garnett Andrews had been successful in life, in business and in law. But even his strong Union sympathies could not save him from the calamity of Reconstruction. Though many did not agree with him, everyone revered and respected the man for his honesty. He was held in the highest esteem. And it was from those heights that Andrews took a devastating fall.

The war had all but wiped out Judge Andrews' financial holdings. His slaves —his servants—were free, and those who remained now had to be paid. Plus, he had taxes to pay to the Union government for the farm. And he knew he needed to find a way to generate income to support his family. Andrews saw the possibilities of using his loyalties to the President to secure a position that would give him the much-needed financial resources.

And why not? He was solidly faithful to the Union, even in the time of secession. Would he not be the best person to serve this President in the back country of Georgia? The choice of Andrews was obvious—to Andrews.

He had thought at first that loyalty would lead to appointment as provisional governor of Georgia in the days following the war. Surely President Johnson would take note of an important former judge and legislator who had renounced secession. But that was not to be. President Johnson had found another suitor.

In late October, in the days following the West murder trial, when Alexander Stephens had returned to his home in Crawfordville from the prison in Massachusetts, Andrews saw another opportunity. He needed a bit of help, and now his old friend Stephens was here to provide it.

Stephens was supportive of Andrews' desire to play a role in Reconstruction and had gone so far as to recommend him to the President for appointment as the federal prosecutor in Georgia. Stephens laid out his endorsement in a letter drafted in early December, while the President was pondering that plea for clemency from Andrews' client, John Brown.

> *Honorable Garnett Andrews of this state informs me that he expects soon to visit Washington on business that may require a personal interview with you. In that event I take pleasure in his behalf in making him known to you by these lines. He is emphatically one of the first men in Georgia. His position for many years upon the Bench in this state kept him from figuring on the national boards. But for talents, ability, integrity and all that gives nobility character he has but few superiors in this or any other state. I have known him personally and intimately for thirty years, and I mean all I say.*

That would seem to be a good enough endorsement on its own. But Stephens went on to promote Andrews' credentials as a Union sympathizer, which may have been more important than his character and life's work.

He was ever a strong Union man—earlier life a Jackson union man— opposed with great ability and that zeal which strong conviction can alone inspire the doctrine of nullification. He was one of the ablest and most efficient advocates of the cause of the union in 1850 and 51. With equal zeal and determination he opposed secession in 1860. He has had nothing to do with the war, I think.

A zealot for the Union! What better commendation for someone to help carry out the president's programs? But Stephens' statement that Andrews had nothing to do with the war was a bit premature, if not misleading, as we shall learn.

Stephens returned to Andrews' legal credentials:

He is an able lawyer, a learned Judge and an upright honest man if ever one lives. I take great pleasure in commending him to your special attention in any matter that he may have to present to you.

Stephens concluded the letter with his signature, but then added a brief postscript that got to the point of the letter:

If the U.S. District attorneyship for this State is not yet filled and Judge Andrews could be induced to accept it I do not think a better appointment could be made.

With Stephens opening the door, Andrews stepped right through, engaging in an exchange of letters and setting up a visit with a powerful congressman, Horace Maynard of Tennessee. An ardent Union supporter, he had served as Johnson's attorney general when he was governor. He was one of the few Southern representatives to keep their seats during the War.

Andrews wrote to the congressman on January 26, 1866, expressing his desire for the presidential appointment and disclosing his current financial challenges. He began the letter by indicating he was still working on a pardon for John Brown.

You ask for testimonials as to loyalty from the first and as to personal and professional character and standing. Enclosed I send copy of a letter of introduction to the President... but I do not care now to risk it by mail as I hope to be able to visit Washington soon and will... have it with me.

The letter needs a little explanation. I had several applications for pardon by my Union friends that I wished to present and also an application for a client who had been condemned by a military commission to be hanged. Besides expecting to be an applicant for the office of District Attorney, I have hence asked for the letter of Mr. Stephens, a copy of which I enclose. Being unable to go to Washington as expected, this letter is—in my hands.

More important to Maynard than why Andrews had delayed his visit was why he was qualified to serve the government. Andrews addresses that:

I have for more than 30 years been writing and speaking against nullification and I have been able to print and send you but three political letters, one of 1851 and two of 1860 out of the many I have written over my own and fictitious signatures. Expecting that you would not attempt to read them I have marked pages that show their character.

Of course, there was more.

...I was a Union man from the beginning; that the first political speech I ever made was against nullification and the last against secession; that I quit the Democrats in 1850 and 51 because they favor secession; never affiliated with any party that was not for the Union, and what I consider the remaining evidence of my loyalty voted for Mr. Toombs once in 50 or 51 because he was the Union man and though living in the same town with him for more than thirty years, it was the first and last time.... I am prepared to share I am not only one of the best, but the best Union man....

Judge Andrews wanted to be actively involved in the politics of Georgia's Reconstruction. He told Maynard some of his friends were urging him to run for the senate. But he feared that could hurt his chances for a presidential appointment—that would come with a salary.

> *Though I have no hope of being elected; I do not care to disappoint my friends if they choose to run me. I fear the election will be over before it will be—for me to accept the crown, if offered. Besides, I have lately learned this office is not but with profit; and having made inquiries in the proper matter, look for information soon that may make me decline the application.*

Yes, money was important to Andrews. He needed some and needed it soon to maintain his family. He wrote he was "mortified" to mention his personal problems to Maynard, but did so anyway, seeing a "humble appointment" as his way out of his current financial predicament.

> *...being of what was an ample fortune for a man of my humble wants and petitions, and with a large and expensive family, I am compelled in my old age to soak away anything that will increase a scrawny income.*

And then Andrews addressed what could be the poison pill to his efforts—his selective support of the Southern war effort.

> *Perhaps, I cannot take the oath so as to qualify for the appointment.— I had two sons in the army and contributed to their support....I also contribute to hospitals and other charities. This I think excusable as an enemy will aid the sick and wounded as an act of mercy.*

With his pitch for the position of federal prosecutor nearly complete, Andrews added a post script:

> *I forgot to say in the right place, though, I am lawyer for forty years, I never practiced in the U.S. Courts.*

Despite his approach through Senator Maynard and Alec Stephens' direct appeal to President Johnson, it was becoming clear that Andrews was not going to receive the appointment he so vigorously sought. But Stephens was not one to abandon a friend. As late as April, he was still trying to help Andrews land somewhere in the federal judiciary.

In another letter to the President, Stephens said in part:

> *I wished also to say something about the appointment of a District Attorney for Georgia—that is an important office—And I wished to present the name of Hon. J. R. Parrot of Cartersville for it—and also the name of Hon. Garnett Andrews for the bench in case the Judiciary system should be revised as proposed.*

As it turned out, despite the help from friends in high places, Andrews never got a federal appointment of any kind. He had even announced for a seat in Congress a few weeks after the West murder trial ended, but that eluded him too. However, with the Radical Republicans taking control of the state government, it would have been unwise to count out the old country lawyer prematurely, as we shall see.

In the midst of Andrews' push for a federal appointment and Brown's and Reese's maneuvering for pardons, Alec Stephens was busy orchestrating his own political resurrection. He remained on friendly terms with President Johnson, who had given him preferential treatment in prison and granted an early parole, enabling Stephens' return to his beloved Liberty Hall in October.

The terms of the parole limited Stephens' activities; the President confined his travels to the state of Georgia. However, in late February, Johnson, at Stephens' request, amended the parole to allow for travel to Washington, D.C., "and such other places in the United States as your business may render necessary...."

But the gentleman from Georgia found himself in a bit of a political pickle in January 1866, when the state convention chose him as U.S. Senator. He knew Johnson would be furious, seeing this as a slap in the face by former Confederates who were infiltrating the state government. Was this Stephens' payback to the Executive who showed him much favor?

Stephens accepted the election out of his loyalty to his beloved Georgia, a decision he tried to temper with Johnson.

I was elected yesterday to the United States Senate by the Georgia Legislature under circumstances particularly embarrassing which will be fully explained by mail.

An effort may be made to impress you with the belief that this was the result of a disposition on the part of the Legislature to oppose the policy of the Administration or the want of a cordial support, and be censured. Such is not the fact—on the contrary my full conviction is that it sprung from an earnest belief whether erroneous or not that it would most effectually aid that policy which is well known I am faithfully laboring to carry out.

But Johnson needn't have worried about the delegation of former Confederates. Congress would take care of them soon enough. Because of their earlier secessionist activities, Stephens and the slate of new federal legislators from Georgia were refused seating.

Although he would not be legislating at the Capitol, Stephens still found a way in. He was summoned to Washington, D.C., by the Congressional Reconstruction Committee to give testimony on the state of affairs in the South at an April 11 hearing.

A couple of weeks prior to his testimony, he wrote to President Johnson, offering to help the administration where he could, but making clear the parameters of that support.

I expected to be in Washington before this time to return you my thanks in person for the enlargement of my parole and to do whatever I could do in the advancement of your policy for restoration, peace and harmony in the country. But the State of my health and the weather, besides the difficulty in raising the means to bear expenses and so forth have delayed the execution of my purpose. I had made all arrangements to get off tomorrow and may do so yet but the sudden change in the weather this morning excites apprehensions that I may not prudently encounter the exposure until the present spell shall pass.

I rush you this line for the purpose of explaining why you have not heard from me since the enlargement of the parole and to let you know that it has not arisen from any want of due appreciation of it. I will also take the occasion to say to you that our legislature before adjournment passed an act in accordance with my advice to them amply I think securing the rights of the Freedmen.

They not only have the right by our law now to contract and be contracted with and to sue and be sued but to testify in our courts in all cases under the same rule that white people are and they are amenable to the same punishments for like offenses as the whites are. No distinctions are made in any of these respects on account of race or color. This it does seem to me should be sufficient.

So far as suffrage is concerned that should be left where the Constitution leaves it with the States. But enough, you will please pardon this. I hope in all events at no distant day to be in Washington.

Stephens arrived in Washington on April 2, and three days later met with Johnson in the Executive Mansion. Did Stephens and Johnson discuss the pardons in the Nellie West murder case? Did Stephens make a personal plea for Andrews' appointment to the federal judiciary? Perhaps, but only they know what transpired.

Stephens went on to appear before the committee, saying he believed the people of Georgia were anxious to assume their former place in the Union. Though the state was accepting emancipation calmly, he asserted, the Legislature was vigorously opposed to the enfranchisement of negroes. The question of suffrage, Stephens believed, constitutionally belonged to the states, as he had stated earlier in his letter to the President.

That Stephens would oppose giving the vote to negroes was not surprising, given the view he had expressed in a major speech in Savannah a month before the war started. The Confederacy's "cornerstone," he argued, "rests upon the great truth that the negro is not equal to the white man; ...slavery, subornation to the superior race, is his natural and normal condition."

Stephens was one of 140 witnesses to appear before the committee. Witness after witness described an unsettled atmosphere across the South between planters and former slaves. Disloyalty was actually widespread, they said, so much so that former Rebels were driving the Unionists from their towns. One minister shared with the committee that "there was a class of boys of 19 or 20 years of age, who would put a Bowie-knife or a bullet through a Northern man, as soon as they would through a mad dog."

But the depravations that befell the freedmen drew the most attention. One of the landowners was asked by a member of Congress why they would murder their own labor force, and he responded, "I cannot answer that in any other way than by supposing it owing to human depravity."

It became obvious to the committee that Stephens' description of political advances in legislative halls was in stark contrast to the state of affairs among the populace.

Following his testimony, as he prepared to leave Washington to return to Georgia, Stephens was summoned to the Executive Mansion by the President on April 16 for an 8 p.m. meeting. But the two men never engaged that night. Stephens explained his absence in a letter to the President the following day.

> *You will please allow me to express my deep regret at not being able to wait longer last night for the desired interview with you for a few minutes only before my leaving the city on my return home. My object was mainly to present to your consideration some views upon the subject of the present condition of the Country so far as relates to the writ of Habeas Corpus and the effect of the late Proclamation on the restoration of that writ....*

Allow me to deeply sympathize with you in the heavy press upon your time. I do not see how you can stand it. With hope, that you may be sustained in your physical strength to bear you through your Herculean work and that your patriotic efforts at restoration of union harmony and prosperity throughout the country may be successful.

I need not repeat the assurance of my cordial and earnest cooperation with you in your exertions whether here or at home. I can remain here no longer [at] present. I must return [home]. With sentiments of the highest consideration and esteem for you personally and officially and best wishes for our Common Country...."

With that explanation, Alec Stephens headed back to Georgia, where he would grow in power and influence, where John Brown and Christopher Reese would be forever unaccountable for the death of Nellie West, and where Garnett Andrews would have to rebuild his finances in ways other than federal patronage.

CHAPTER 21

———⬩———

Crawfordville, Georgia
March 28, 1883

"THAT IS QUITE A STORY—THE West murder—and how Reese and Brown did in fact get away with murder," I remarked to Josiah. "It's hard to imagine how such a calculated killing could be just swept away by political connections through the stroke of a pen."

"I told you that justice in the South works in strange ways." A broad smile came across Josiah's face—a smile I had seen many times during our discussions.

Today we moved our meeting from that lovely setting at Liberty Hall to a dark and foul-smelling tavern adjacent to the hotel where I was staying. Why, I wondered.

"I know you are probably wondering why I told you to meet me here," my host said as we seated ourselves at a table in a corner of the room. The focal point of the place was a long polished pine-wood bar that extended the length of one wall. Behind it were shelves of bottles and glasses surrounding a large mirror hanging in the middle. Several tables dotted the dimly lit room.

A tall woman in a red polka dot dress approached our table. "Can I get you gentlemen something?"

"Coffee," I responded.

"A shot of rye and water is fine for me," Josiah chimed in. If I've learned one thing from my companion, it's that a shot of spirits will get his storytelling going.

She took her leave, and I dove right into the conversation. "Yes, I am quite interested why you wanted to meet me here."

"This, Mister Wood, is where the story picks up."

Now, I was a bit confused. I had thought the story was over. I was planning to start my trip back north on the afternoon train. Had already thought about how I would write the facts of Nellie's murder and Stephens' manipulations into a newspaper story.

"Brown and Reese didn't hang, as we have learned. But we also know they didn't spend much time in jail either. At least Brown didn't. He lived for about a year after his release and died late in 1866." I nodded as I entered the information into my notebook.

"He stayed in Raytown. Don't know how he met his demise. The family kept his passing rather quiet."

"Now Reese," Josiah continued, "he's a different story."

"Please tell," I begged.

"We all thought C.C. would get his life straight after being spared the hangman's noose. He moved back onto the family farm. Seems to have stayed out of trouble, and in April 1868 he married a young lady—no, not the woman you are thinking about, Mister Wood."

Yes, I thought he had collected on the offer from Brown to marry his stepdaughter, Caroline, and collect $5 to boot. Or, maybe even the $500 he had offered while in jail.

"How so?" I asked.

"He married Julia Littleton before the justice of the peace here in Taliaferro County. Times being what they were, they moved in with his parents on their farm. Settled in and tended to the crops, they did."

Josiah added, in case there was ever any doubt, "And Julia, she's quite a looker. She fancies herself as a fine dresser, preferring silks and lace and such."

"Not quite the image of a farmer's wife?"

"I would say not!" Josiah liked to embellish his descriptions, and this time was no different. "With those clothes, her golden hair and her soft features, I picture her in a more sophisticated setting. But she must have seen something in C.C. that the rest of us missed. Anyway, she was about a year older than C.C. Wasn't long before they had the baby girl."

"As for Caroline," he continued, "she found her an older man, Robert Kendrick, who had some children of his own. They married in Taliaferro County in 1868, a couple of months after Christopher and Julia married. She actually got the better end of the deal. Robert went on to serve in the state legislature. Christopher Reese? Well, that's why we're here."

Our drinks were delivered while Josiah was recapturing the nuptials. He quickly took a sip, and the story began to unfold. I leaned back in my chair a bit to get comfortable.

"We're in this tavern today because it is the scene of the next important chapter of Christopher's life. This one, too, held deadly consequences."

I could already see myself extending my stay in Crawfordville. This story seemed to have no end. But surely there must be one.

"See, over there on the floor by the bar?" Josiah got up, walked over to near the bar and pointed to the floor.

Two other men at another table began to watch him.

"That's where the killing happened, you know," one of the men said in a very loud voice.

Josiah looked back over their way and pointed a finger at them. "Now you guys just hush. You're messing with my story!"

"Sorry Mister Stephens," the other said. "My friend didn't mean no harm. Mind if we listen in?"

"That's quite all right," he replied. "Mister Wood, that stain you see on the floor...." He again pointed his finger down toward the floor. I was struggling to make out what he was talking about. He continued, "That stain is blood. It's another reminder of Christopher Reese, a reminder of his wickedness."

Josiah returned to his seat at the table, while the two men at the other table turned their chairs to hear better. "So, let me take you back to July of 1869...."

Crawfordville, Georgia
July 24, 1869

The tavern at the rear of the hotel on Crawfordville's main thoroughfare was the local watering hole. A place men could gather to share tales true and imagined. Where visitors and strangers could take a respite from their travels. In many ways it was the center of life for Crawfordville. Only don't tell the local preachers that, even though one or more have occasioned its inviting atmosphere.

One of the regulars who stopped in on July 24 was Christopher C. Reese. He began to drink, "as is his custom," we are told. He was somewhat of a celebrated citizen among the whites still bitter over the war. They liked to trade stories with him about his days riding with the Confederate Cavalry. "C.C., you ever kill a Yankee?" Talk like that. Reese loved the attention and enjoyed sharing tales real and imagined.

He also was none too kind to the negroes in town. His bitterness toward them had only grown because the death of a crippled old negro woman nearly sent him to the gallows. "Best everyone stays with their own kind," he might have said. On this hot summer day, Reese's "own kind" was the bottle.

This time of the year also weighed heavily on Reese. Four years ago this month he killed Nellie West, an event that still haunted him in the deepest places in his mind.

We don't know what Reese was drinking or how many drinks he had had, but there was no question he was feeling his oats. A friend of his, one-time school teacher Thomas Edwards, was in the tavern at the same time. Edwards, a father of eight children, was, according to those who knew him, "a quiet, peaceable man," though "he drank like everything." Edwards had a view of negroes different from that of his younger acquaintance. Members of his family were farmers and former slave holders, but Edwards understood the wrongness of treating their wards harshly.

During the war, Reese signed up for the fight; Thomas, on the other hand, snared a Justice of the Peace appointment with the help of his father's political influence, thus keeping him from being conscripted. Thomas eventually did join the state guard and saw some action at the Battle of Jonesboro, outside Atlanta, before returning home on sick leave.

Nearly four years to the day after Nellie West was murdered, Edwards brought a young colored boy into the tavern with him to buy the boy some candy. Reese took issue with Edwards' friendly gesture. He also got visibly upset that Thomas would have the nerve to bring the boy into what Reese considered a white establishment.

"Nigger lover!" Reese shouted to Edwards.

Others in the bar were taken aback, knowing that the two men were actually good friends. Maybe their friendship was solid enough to withstand even harsh insults. Some friendships can endure, if the liquor doesn't get in the way.

Edwards turned his head to face Reese, and they began arguing. Finally, Edwards had had enough of his brash young friend and turned to walk away.

Reese reached into his belt, pulled out his pistol and raised it chest high to threaten Edwards, saying, "I could just shoot your heart out."

The unarmed Edwards made no threats or demonstrations in response. He was probably more puzzled than anything. He turned back to face Reese.

Two men who moments ago had been enjoying the finest spirits the tavern had to offer were now face-to-face, only about five feet apart. Reese with pistol drawn.

Reese pulled back the hammer. The revolver clicked as the cylinder locked into place. Others in the tavern, too reluctant to intervene between fighting friends, slipped away. So did the young negro lad at Edward's urging.

In response to Reese's threat, Edwards opened his shirt, and as a brave man will do, or as a fool who has had too much to drink will do, told him to "shoot."

Reese obliged him. There was no hesitation like he had shown in shooting Nellie four years earlier. No further prompting was needed. "Just shoot," Edwards challenged.

The shot sounded like an explosion in the confines of the tavern, with the sound reverberating for what seemed like at least a full minute. The ball entered Edwards' chest near his heart, and he instantly dropped to the floor.

As the smoke cleared, Reese stood in silent disbelief of what he had just done to his friend. There was no mistaking he had shot him, but had he killed him?

The answer would come in just moments. With his blood, bright red, draining through his now-stained blue shirt and pooling around him on the wooden floor by the bar, Edwards took his last breath.

"My God," Reese exclaimed, "I have just killed my best friend!"

To anyone else, this might have been a sobering moment, but to Reese, it only fueled the rage built up in his angry soul. With pistol in hand, he ran out of the tavern and spent the next several hours on the streets of Crawfordville, threatening anyone who would attempt to arrest him. No one tried.

He then fled town. Not for the safety and comfort of his wife and his family's farm. No, Christopher Reese was a man on the run hightailing it down the road to parts unknown.

The search for him spread beyond Crawfordville and east Georgia. Where could he have gone? Governor Rufus Bullock was eager to help find out. At the governor's direction, the state posted a $1,000 cash reward for Reese's capture.

News of the murder had to be particularly unsettling to Alexander Stephens, whose Liberty Hall was so close to the tavern that he might have even heard the fatal shot when it was fired. For Alec, the untimely affair had two victims: his friend Thomas Edwards and the boy he had spared from execution only a handful of years earlier.

At the time of the killing, Stephens was confined to his home as the result of a horrible accident that had occurred a few months earlier. While walking along Raytown Road about a mile from Liberty Hall, he was severely injured when he took hold of a large iron gate opening on a pasture he wished to cross.

Stephens did not note that the gate was only leaning against the posts. He tugged on it, and it fell on him. He managed to crawl out from underneath, and even got halfway home on foot. A wagon was summoned to take him the rest of the way.

By that summer he was no longer confined to bed. He could sit up for four or five hours a day in a chair. But his left hip was badly injured, and in spite of sulfur baths, steam baths and various kinds of manipulations that he tried at one time or another, he was unable to move about unless he used crutches or a roller chair. He was never able to walk again without assistance.

But there is no doubt, regardless of his physical condition, Stephens remained mentally alert and would be following this murder case very closely.

With a substantial reward at stake, the search for Christopher Reese intensified. A thousand dollars was a small fortune at the time. Reason enough to join the hunt.

Reese stayed on the loose for about two months, but his luck finally ran out in late September in Alabama.

Short on friends and supporters, Reese turned to the man he considered his one true friend, the man who had helped him through his last brush with the grim reaper. He turned to someone who had already proven to him that he had the power of salvation on earth.

On September 29, 1869, Alexander Stephens received the following telegram from a jail in Alabama: "*Will employ you as my council. Am arrested. Confined jail. C.C. Reese.*"

Reese was brought back from Alabama and housed in the jailhouse in Augusta. A court order was issued for that arrangement because of fears for his life if he were held in the jail in Crawfordville.

The Augusta jail was familiar to Reese. He and John Brown had spent half a year there while the earlier murder case was decided. But this time he would become even more familiar with it, waiting there almost two years for his case to come to trial.

And that trial finally did begin on June 6, 1871, before a jury in a courtroom in Hancock County. There would be no military commission this time. With the seating on February 1, 1871, of U.S. Sen. Jonah Hill, war powers in Georgia concluded with the formal closing of the Military District of Georgia. Justice was again the sole providence of the State of Georgia.

Reese was put on trial in the courthouse in the town of Sparta because the defense believed an impartial jury could not be found in Taliaferro County. There was probably a lot of truth to that idea since both the killer and victim had well-known reputations, but not for the same reasons.

Reese had sent that telegram Alec Stephens asking for his help once again by serving as his attorney. While Stephens' law practice was quite active at the time, he would not be representing Christopher Reese. That responsibility fell to John Alexander Stephens, the son of Alec's half-brother Linton.

The presiding judge in the case was no stranger to Reese. He had seen him many times in the jails in Washington and Augusta and had sat at the table next to him during a two-week military commission trial in Washington. The now-presiding Superior Court Judge was Garnett Andrews, returned to the bench by appointment of Governor Rufus Bullock.

The trial itself lasted only two days. On June 8, 1871, Christopher Reese stood before the jury and Judge Andrews to hear the unanimous verdict read by jury foreman A. B. Buckner: "We the jury find this defendant guilty."

Yes, he had heard correctly. Guilty of murdering his friend Thomas Edwards. Now what would happen to him? Surely Judge Andrews would look favorably on him. Would he recall the facts from the military commission, that Reese had issued a second confession that had exonerated Andrews' client? Would there not be some compensation or consideration for that? Would Andrews remember the appeal to Reese's "youth and inexperience"? Was he to be sentenced to the gallows a second time?

Certainly, all of this weighed on the aging jurist. But Andrews knew the law and knew that crimes have consequence. He knew the killer as a youthful hothead, and he knew the victim to be a well-respected citizen. He had also just heard the jury unanimously agree on Reese's complicity. Judge Andrews crafted his order with all the legal acumen he could muster.

> *The defendant at this term of said Superior Court of Hancock County having been put on his trial…and by a legal and proper jury found guilty of the crime of murder and no sufficient cause to the contrary having been shown, it is the order, judgment and sentence of this court for the convict Columbus Reese… that the Sheriff …is ordered to take the convict to the County of Taliaferro and on a gallows…to be erected within one side of the courthouse of said County of Taliaferro he is ordered and commanded on the fourth day of August next between the hours of one and four o'clock PM on that day publicly to hang said convict by the neck until he is dead.*

In those days public hangings took place on the lot north of the courthouse square in Crawfordville. These were community events, bringing in folks from the village as well as from far out in the countryside. The people could see final justice delivered in an atmosphere that was much like a town festival, with food vendors and others selling their wares. Music was never out of place.

It was not enough for Andrews simply to pronounce that Reese would be executed. He also dictated instructions on how the execution would be carried out.

> *And it is further ordered that the said convict be suspended by the neck as aforesaid for the space and time of thirty minutes and until a practicing*

physician of said County of Taliaferro shall pronounce that death has occurred; that it is further ordered that when it shall have been so pronounced that said convict is dead the Sheriff of Taliaferro County is ordered to deliver his body to his relatives or friends on their demand and if not so demanded, he is ordered to bury it at the expense of said County of Taliaferro.

Judge Andrews spared no quarter with Reese. If there had been any feelings of sympathy for the lad lingering from the earlier trial, none were in evidence here. Andrews' reputation would have demanded nothing less.

CHAPTER 22

Common Jail
Augusta, Georgia
Summer 1871

REESE NEEDED A LIFE LINE and he needed it fast. Two years of sitting in the dank confines of the jail in Augusta awaiting his execution was taking its toll, both physically and mentally. "I am very feeble," Reese wrote. "I eat nothing. I cannot eat. Such as we have is very gross." He might blame the food, and rightfully so, but it was a good bet he was coming to the realization that he was trapped in a death spiral with no escape.

As was the case with most prisoners, Reese was being reintroduced to his maker. "I have religious interviews every day," he wrote. Perhaps his religious education had included the verse from Psalms that best summed up his current predicament: *"Have mercy upon me, O Lord, for I am in trouble: mine eye is consumed with grief, yea, my soul and my belly."* Psalm 31:9

Christopher Reese may not have been remorseful, but he was certainly resourceful. He remembered the Stephens family had helped him out of one jam, so why not turn again to Alec? His political influence had only grown in the half dozen years since release from federal custody. Yes, a word from Mr. Stephens to the right person would help, Reese thought.

So, on June 12, four days after receiving his death sentence, Reese did something similar to what he had done when he was in this same fix for killing the freedwoman. It was time for another jailhouse confession. This time in his own hand. No jailers or witnesses to take down his statement. This time it would be a very personal letter to Stephens.

Seated at a table in his dimly lit cell, Reese began his letter by describing his circumstances. Not surprisingly, he claimed he was the victim of those circumstances.

> *Again it has fell my lot to be doomed to death by the way of great misfortune. Not from the affects of an indignant heart has this unpleasant sentence been pronounced upon me, but through great misfortune from childhood days in which acts has been habituated in me....*

You have to wonder what childhood habits would turn someone into a killer. Why his misfortune would be worse than the misfortune he delivered upon his two victims and their families. But more startling was Reese's selective amnesia about what he had done.

> *Though I feel as sane as any man, though I have been accused of things that I have no recollection of, and what passed the day of Mr. Edwards death, I am unable to say. For I remember what only as I have been told and God alone knows my innocence of this crime which I am as suffer death for...that I had shot my dear friend Mr. Edwards who I loved as a brother and God knows...*

Reese's arguments were not cut from whole cloth. President Johnson's Judge Advocate General Joseph Holt saw right through those delusions in his arguments to the President on three occasions to uphold the original death sentence in 1865. That Reese could cloak himself in a claim of innocence six years later went beyond rational thinking. His words betrayed the genuine fear that obviously now possessed him.

He knew Stephens had the connections to save him from certain death. Stephens had saved him once; would he do it again? And why not explain that the elder statesman would not be doing this for Reese himself, but for the sake of his wife and the parents he knew Stephens was close to?

> *I wish to say to you as my friend to use your influence to have this honorable sentence commuted to imprisonment for the sake of a poor heartbroken wife and mother not as I feel a dread of death. I wish God…takes that stain from a respectable family that gave me birth.*

Reese went on to write that he was a changed person who desired to use a friendship with Stephens and his considerable influence to avoid the "pain of death."

> *You have been my true friend in my other misfortunes and my regard to you for it is inexplicable and if you will help me in this I promise you in the name of a omnipotent god that I shall live a Christian life to the end of my days and keep myself from all bad…I should not fail to do it justice for the salvation of my soul. I hope you will extend your influence for me and see what can be done. I have but a few days in this world if not a change soon and I hope you will succeed in taking from me this excruciating and ignominious pain of death that had been administered upon me. I feel that your influence with the official powers will be heeded. And I send my wife to you that you may give her such advice as will be necessary in my case.*
>
> *I can't say what good a politician will do…. I will be glad to hear from you by the mail. I pray God you will not desert me in this trying hour of despair. I hope to hear soon. God's blessings ever attend you in this life.*

Reese had given it his best shot. Even though he did not accept direct responsibility for Thomas Edwards' murder or show any measure of remorse, he nonetheless believed that Alexander Stephens could and would once again boldly intercede on his behalf.

Governor Rufus Bullock alone had the power to stop this execution, as he had done for so many others facing death sentences. So many pardons, in fact, that the state legislature had begun asking questions about his use of that power. But for Reese, time was of the essence. He alone was powerless to stop the executioner's clock as it wound down, but he knew Stephens and Bullock could put the brakes on it.

Days went by after Reese wrote his letter. Days turned to weeks. He had plenty of time to ponder what he had done and how he might escape the judgment for it. Those who knew him also anticipated the outcome. Would the public hanging of the troubled youth from Raytown be a summer spectacle in Crawfordville? They wondered.

Then the word came in mid-July. Just a month ahead of the day of reckoning for Reese—and the day of justice for the Edwards family. The governor addressed Reese's appeal in a brief executive order. Bullock was willing to postpone the execution for two months to give time for further study of the facts. Bullock's wording was purely legal-speak and gave no hint of what he was thinking for a final outcome.

Whereas Columbus C. Reese convicted of the crime of murder has been sentenced by the Judge of the Superior Court…to be executed by hanging by the neck until dead on Friday, the 20th day of August, and

Whereas, application has been made to me to reshape the sentence upon said Columbus C. Reese, and to postpone his execution that time may be given for the development and presentation of important facts.

Therefore I, Rufus J. Bullock, Governor of said state do hereby suspend the execution of the said sentence upon the said Columbus C. Reese until Friday, October 27, 1871 between the hours of 10 o'clock in the forenoon and 2 o'clock in the afternoon, and I command you to withhold from the execution the said Columbus C. Reese until the day and between the hours of the aforesaid.

Clearly, the State was not yet through with Reese. Was hanging inevitable, or would the governor see the crime differently than the 12 jurors in Hancock County and Judge Andrews had seen it? Reese had put his trust in Alexander H. Stephens and God, not necessarily in that order. He had reason enough to hope for a favorable outcome.

As he sat in his Augusta jail cell awaiting his return to Crawfordville and execution, Christopher Columbus Reese prepared to meet his maker. He had not previously been known as a religious man. Far from it. But now, facing death, he found comfort in a message of peace and forgiveness. He had engaged himself in religious instruction. And there in the lockup, he was baptized and joined the Catholic Church, perhaps bringing some measure of comfort.

As the October execution date approached, Reese was moved to the jail in Taliaferro County. There he would prepare for the end of his life and be available for visits by his wife and parents. In that jail, in the shadow of the gallows, he awaited any response from Governor Bullock to his plea and the pleas of others. And he speculated whether Alec Stephens had enough influence to sway the governor.

More weeks went by, and the agony of the wait continued for Reese. Edwards' family members no doubt shared an agony of their own while awaiting the outcome.

And perhaps, watching from afar were a family of freedmen, the West family, praying that the courts were about to deliver the justice they had been denied.

Asking Governor Bullock for a pardon was not an unusual request in Reconstruction Georgia. In fact during the three years he was in office, the New York native and former Augusta railroad executive issued a total of 523 pardons. That may have been good news for those who escaped the judgments of the courts, but the practice was not well received by the Legislature, which formed a committee to investigate.

The governor's Executive Secretary, Robert H. Atkinson, managed the pardon requests for the office. His primary role was to prepare the salient points of the testimony for review by the Governor. Bullock frequently endorsed Atkinson's recommendations based solely on the evidence presented, either for or against the pardon.

The legislative committee found that no standard for an independent review appeared to exist. The committee concluded that Bullock indiscriminately granted pardons. Further the committee reported, "Money could get pardons. Some of the governor's staff had a pardon brokerage. Pardoning before conviction was a favorite practice." Also, when recommendations for pardon were made by members of the Legislature, or other prominent officials, the pardons were generally granted as a matter of course. "Bullock sinned broad gauge..." the committee wrote.

Secretary Atkinson, who had distinguished himself in the Army of Northern Virginia, serving under Gen. Robert E. Lee, sought to defend the governor's actions. Many of those 500 pardons were related to indictments returned before or during the war, he argued, "and pardons were only granted upon the solicitation of the most well-known and respectable citizens of the counties from which said convicts were sentenced."

One pardon in particular had drawn the ire of Reese's neighbors in Washington, Georgia. Just a few months before Reese's conviction for the Edwards murder, Judy Heard, a colored woman, was before Judge V. M. Barns on a charge of using "obscene and vulgar words in the presence of a female." Barns, a Bullock appointee to the bench, sentenced Heard to a $25 fine or 30 days in jail. Not having any funds, Judy Heard was locked up.

The governor's office ordered the woman released, claiming there was no evidence the other woman actually had heard the words Judy used. Heard had been illegally and erroneously convicted, the governor would have folks believe, based solely on a statement submitted outside the court by a friend of hers. One writer questioned, "How can His Excellency expect the people of Georgia to be law-abiding and appeal to the courts to punish offenders, when he stands ready with his pardons to wash away the stains of crime as fast as the courts can convict?"

Bullock was no fan of the Reconstruction legislature, which was dominated by former Confederates. He rejected the committee's criticisms of his use of the power of pardon outright, telling the lawmakers in part, "...there is no testimony showing anything corrupt in the exercise of executive clemency on my part." And he challenged the committee to put forward even a single pardon "obtained through corrupt or improper influence."

Bullock concluded his defense by saying, "The most that can therefore be said against me is that I erred in judgment, and listened too easily to the promptings of mercy."

But issuing pardons was the least of the Radical Republican Governor's problems with the Legislature. He was under constant attack and threatened with impeachment—even criminal charges—on an array of issues, including dishing political favors to his cronies building the state's railroad network.

Even General Toombs would observe that Bullock had "committed a hundred offenses, any one of which is sufficient to convict him. The trouble with the fellow," Toombs observed, "is that he don't know half the time when he does wrong."

Bullock firmly believed that the state House would vote out articles of impeachment, even without a formal investigation, and the Senate would go so far as to unseat a number of Republican senators sufficient to secure a conviction regardless of the truth or validity of the charges.

The political pot was boiling, and Bullock sincerely believed he would be the main course at a good old Southern barbeque. A writer for the venerated *Atlanta Constitution* described Bullock's three years in office this way: "The man made and unmade Legislatures, toyed with the State's sacred sovereignty like a worthless bauble, swayed the judiciary, and scattered the people's money with the liberality of a prince and the reckless caprice of a munificent madman."

On October 23, 1871, four days before the scheduled execution of Christopher Reese, Bullock made a tactical decision. He chose to step aside, issuing a brief written message:

Be it known, that good and sufficient reasons, me thereunto moving, I do hereby resign the office of Governor of this State to take effect Monday next, the 30ᵗʰ day of October, and on that day and date deliver over to the Honorable Benjamin Conley, President of the Senate, the Executive powers of the Government until the election and qualification of a Governor.

The abrupt departure had served the governor and the legislature well, but what about Reese? He was now just within days of hanging, and the person who had held the key to his freedom was preparing to flee the state. Had all hope been lost? Had Alexander Stephens run out of influence? Surely, if the investigative committee's report on pardons was correct, a request for pardon from someone as influential as Stephens would have been a matter of routine. Or, so it would seem.

On October 23, Bullock's letter of resignation would not be the only bit of unfinished business he would address. Not by a long shot. He had not forgotten the request he had received months earlier from Stephens—that plea to spare the life of the young man from Raytown.

There the answer was, tucked away in the minutes kept by Executive Secretary Atkinson of the business conducted by the governor on that fall day.

Whereas C.C. Reese was tried for and convicted of the crime of murder and was therefore sentenced by the judge to be executed by hanging by the neck until dead on the 20ᵗʰ day of August.

Whereas, an application made, an order granting a reprieve to the said Reese until the 27ᵗʰ day of October was filed on the 15ᵗʰ day of July last by this Department for the purpose of giving time for the development and presentation of important facts.

Yes, the governor knew who Reesc was and what he faced. He also knew time was running out to address the concerns raised by his friend Alec. Stephens was not the only one in Taliaferro County to come to Reese's defense. Petitions to the President had saved the man's sad life once, so why not petitions to the governor?

> *Whereas a petition has been presented to me signed by citizens of Taliaferro County embracing the names of all classes of citizens praying for a commutation of the sentence of capital punishment imposed upon the said Reese to imprisonment in the penitentiary for life, on the ground that grave doubts exist as to whether or not the said Reese was laboring under a mental aberration when he committed the said homicide.*

Was Reese of a sound mind when he shot Tom Edwards? He had told Stephens in his jailhouse plea that he didn't remember killing his friend; he knew only what he had been told. But those 12 citizens in Hancock County had no doubt when they, as the jury, voted unanimously to convict him. Oh, but this is Southern justice, and we have not heard the last from the jurors themselves. They've been signing petitions too.

> *Whereas in addition to the twelve jurors before whom the said Reese was tried and who earnestly join in the prayer of the petitioners aforesaid, the Honorable Alexander Stephens recommends the exercise of Executive Clemency in behalf of the condemned, he being of the opinion that the ends of justice and the object of humanity would be best attained by a commutation of the punishment of death, to that of close imprisonment in the petitionary for life.*

So, the tide was turning in favor of Reese. His friend Alec, the jurors who convicted him and his many supporters in the community had all come together to plead for his life. Not for pardon, but for his life. A life to be lived in prison. A commutation. And the lame duck governor obliged:

> *Now, therefore, in consideration of the facts and circumstances aforesaid, and believing that the majesty of the court will be fully vindicated by*

commuting the said sentence as recommended by the petitioner. I, Rufus J. Bullock, Governor of said State by virtue of the powers and authority in me vested by the Constitution and Laws of this State, do hereby commute the said sentence of capital punishment imposed upon C.C. Reese to imprisonment in the penitentiary of this State for and during the term of his natural life, and it is hereby Ordered that the Principal Keeper of said penitentiary forthwith cause the said C.C. Reese to be conveyed and confined in said penitentiary in pursuance of and in compliance with the commuted sentence aforesaid.

Southern justice takes strange turns, indeed. Christopher Columbus Reese now would know that oh too well. Not once, but twice.

Twice Reese was tried for killing people he had no reason to be at odds with, twice he was convicted by independent panels for murder, and twice was sentenced to death. Twice Alexander H. Stephens used his influence to reverse the course of justice. Twice Reese was given a second chance to live. And twice Reconstruction justice failed the families of victims of his crimes.

——◆——

Crawfordville, Georgia
March 1883
"Mister Wood, we are nearing the end of our story," Josiah revealed.

I was beginning to think otherwise. So were the two guys at the other table who had been listening in.

"On October 27th, Reese was once again returned from Crawfordville to the jail in Augusta. There he would await his transfer into state custody and begin serving his life sentence." Josiah asked the waitress for another round, so I knew there had to be more.

"He would not spend the months and years ahead in a cell on a soft mattress, Mister Wood. No…at age twenty-five, Christopher Reese would begin a new life of hard labor in service to the industrial barons who were laying railroad lines to prosperity," Josiah said.

"And why was that?" I took his bait.

"In those days, there were no prisons in which to serve such an indefinite sentence. They had been destroyed during the war. What the state did with people like Reese was lease them out for just pennies a day to the companies building Governor Bullock's Reconstruction legacy, either by laying track for new railroad lines or digging in the state's primitive mines."

"That certainly wasn't much of a future for anyone," I remarked.

"Sir, you are correct. Although convict labor was not unheard of prior to the war, it flourished during Reconstruction," Josiah responded. "In 1866 the Legislature allowed the governor to lease out the prisoners to private companies. Governor Bullock signed contracts to lease inmates to his political and business friends for as little as ten dollars a year."

"And how did that go over?" I asked.

"The state liked the system because it was profitable, and business liked it because it was a source of cheap labor." With a fresh glass in hand, Josiah continued.

"But such a system was ripe for abuse, as would be expected. An investigation by Legislators in 1870 exposed convicts working ten to sixteen hours a day in inadequate conditions. Whippings by leather straps embedded with brass rivets were a common means to keep inmates obedient."

"Sounds a lot like slavery to me."

"Mister Wood, the system had all the trappings of slavery but made no distinction between negro and white."

"And what happened to Reese?"

"He was sent to northeast Georgia to work on the Georgia Air-Line Railroad. He had exchanged the hangman's noose for the promise of a lifetime of grading, blasting and laying track in perilous conditions and environments."

"Something tells me that this tale does not end so cleanly, Josiah."

"And you would be right, sir," replied Josiah. "The irony of Christopher's incarceration is quite amazing, even to me. You see, to oversee the inmate population, the state appointed what was known as a Principal Keeper. He would periodically inspect the condition of the inmates on behalf of the state government and record his findings.

"The Principal Keeper monitoring C.C. Reese's work camp was named—John Brown." A broad smile crept across Josiah's face with this revelation.

"And what happened to Reese?" I again inquired.

"He served a mere two years of his life sentence," Josiah said. I feared another long lesson coming on Southern justice and yet another story about a pardon.

"This time, not even Uncle Alec could affect the outcome of final justice, Mister Wood. An obscure entry in an inmate log book records Christopher's death in a railroad work camp on January 20, 1873."

"What happened to him?"

"That, Mister Wood, is where our story must end, for the circumstances of his demise were never recorded."

———

March 29, 1883

On the train ride back to Atlanta, I had time to reflect on my time in Crawfordville and the lurid story that had been shared with me by the affable Josiah Stephens. I thought about how I would frame the telling of this tormented tale of murder and betrayal in a way that would be of interest to my readers. How justice failed not one family, but two—the loved ones of Nellie West and Thomas Edwards. How power and influence would so easily trump fairness and equity. No, never in my career have I come across a tale infected by so many wicked hands. And, never in my career have I come across a story that cried out so loudly and mournfully for a hero.

EPILOGUE

May 1907

SOME TWO DOZEN YEARS HAVE passed since I wrote the story of how Alexander Stephens worked to spare the life of Christopher Reese. And many times since I first heard the account, I have revisited in my memory the people involved, those I had come to know so well by reputation. The perpetrators, the victims, the families, those responsible for administering justice—they all represent a collective perversion of the basic precept of our Constitution that guarantees justice for all.

I was never able to determine Stephens' motivations for becoming engaged in this sordid affair, other than his sense of loyalty—Stephens' loyalty to long-time friends, white friends at that. But I suspect there is much more to it.

Stephens treated his own slaves with deference and kindness. Yet, before the war, he had spoken of slavery as the bedrock of the Confederacy and publicly argued that whites were superior to negroes. With that point of view, it could reasonably be argued that Stephens' loyalty was based on race more than relationships.

Which is more important: loyalty or justice? You might say the correct answer is: "It depends." It's a given that our nation's system of justice is not fair to all, but does that mean we should not at least try to keep the scales of Lady Justice balanced? Surely that is possible.

Josiah Stephens and I have kept up our correspondence. He's married now with twins and presides as a judge on the Georgia Superior Court. He is a well-respected jurist whose opinions are frequently cited in complicated cases. I enjoy reading his musings that at times arrive at my office with a bottle of homebrew from Liberty Hall. I also retain fond memories of my time with him in Crawfordville and long ago ceased cursing the editor who sent me there. The many simple life lessons Josiah imparted to me—while I was rocking in a chair on the porch of a beautiful mansion in rural Georgia with a glass of corn liquor in my hand—I still hold dear.

Over the years I've tried to keep up with some of the folks who played a role in this incredible story. Sadly, many had died before I made their acquaintance.

Of course we know John Brown's death in Raytown, Georgia, was recorded in a family Bible on November 6, 1867. We don't know how he died. Maybe it was divine intervention, like what happened to Bob Lampkin, one of the meanest slave owners in Richmond County, Georgia. They say Lampkin beat his own slaves and any others he found in the road. He was so mean that the negroes believed God actually let him freeze to death. "He come to town and got drunk, and when he was going back home in his buggy, he froze stiff going up Rae's Creek Hill. White and colored was glad when he died."

On January 20, 1873, Christopher Reese died in the prison work camp in northeast Georgia. How he died we'll never know. We do know the railroad line he worked on was completed by 1873 but went broke the following year.

Seven months later, on August 14, 1873, Judge Garnett Andrews died at his home in Washington, Georgia. An obituary described him as *"superior in everything, except trickery and demagoguism."*

On July 31, 1875, the man who had enabled Reese to escape the grip of death, President Andrew Johnson, died of a stroke while visiting his daughter in Tennessee. A *New York Times* obituary concluded, *"He was always headstrong and 'sure he was right' even in his errors."*

The following year on March 15, Rev. Mansfield French died at his home in Pearsall, Long Island, New York, after retiring from his ministry and mission work. From an obituary, *"He survived the oblivion of all the aspersions malicious partisans cast upon him during the war and passed away in the confidence and love of all his brethren."*

John Brown's co-counsel, Col. John Weems, went on to serve as Secretary of the Georgia State Senate, then as a judge in Macon. He died in Macon, Georgia, on November 30, 1876.

On March 4, 1883, Alexander H. Stephens died at his home, Liberty Hall, in Crawfordville, Georgia, following an extended illness. Stephens had written in his diary on July 13, 1865: *"If the real truth of history in relation to the Southern Cause shall ever be written, it will be to this effect: The Southern mind was influenced and misguided by a class of public men, politicians not statesmen, newspaper editors, and preachers, who possessed far more ambition and zeal than wisdom and knowledge."*

In Colombia, South America, on August 28, 1891, Gen. Edward Wild died while surveying a railroad line. A close friend, John W. Chandler, described him as *"a marked and original character, true to his convictions on all occasions, the personification of devotion to principle."*

President Johnson's trusted legal advisor, Judge Advocate Gen. Joseph Holt, who argued vigorously for execution for Brown and Reese, died on August 1, 1894, during a peaceful retirement in Washington, D.C. In a special publication on the Lincoln conspirators' trial, the *Philadelphia Daily Inquirer* said, General Holt *"needs no eulogy. His reputation as a lawyer is known throughout the nation."*

Reese's attorney in the West murder case, Samuel Barnett, died on March 23, 1896. After the trial he helped craft the Freedmen's Code of Georgia, became the state's first Railroad Commissioner and was editor of an Augusta newspaper. He was remembered as *"one of the most rounded, philosophical, and varied men of letters and affairs that Georgia has had."*

And just last month, on April 22, Governor Rufus Bullock died in Albion, New York. He went back to Georgia, was acquitted at trial and became a leading citizen in Atlanta. *The Atlanta Constitution* praised him this way: *"Few Georgians, whether by birth or adoption, did more real good for the state than he."*

I have failed to record the final outcome of the West family members, not by neglect, but because the information cannot be found. The West family members appear to have vanished into the air like the steam rising from the spout of a hot tea kettle. Perhaps, at some point they enjoyed their freedom by moving on from the West farm and changing their names.

We have to ask ourselves: If there had been no secession, if there had been no Civil War, if there had been no Reconstruction, how would things have been different? That's a tough question that I will leave to others to ponder.

What I do know is this: The war and post-war periods will be studied and examined for generations to come. Politicians and generals on both sides will be revered and glorified beyond their due. And recriminations from slavery will continue to eat away at our country's moral fabric.

Nellie West was a champion. She may not have felt like one at the time, but freedwoman Adeline Willis of Wilkes County clearly understood the impact this simple but strong woman had on her and so many others:

> *We niggers wouldn't know nothing about it at all if it hadn't been for a little old black, sassy woman in the Quarters that was talking' all the time about 'freedom.' She give our white folks trouble—she was so sassy to them, but they didn't sell her and she was set free along with us.*

ADDITIONAL READING

For additional reading on the people and events described in this book, please see the following:

Andrews, Eliza Frances. *The War-Time Journal of a Georgia Girl 1864-1865.* U of Nebraska P, 1997.

Andrews, Garnett. *Reminiscences of an Old Georgia Lawyer.* Franklin Steam, 1870.

Casstevens, Frances H. *Edward A. Wild and the African Brigade in the Civil War.* McFarland, 2003.

---. *Tales from the North and the South.* McFarland, 2007.

Cimbala, Paul A. *Under the Guardianship of the Nation: The Freedmen's Bureau and the Reconstruction of Georgia 1865-1870.* U of Georgia P, 2003.

Conway, Alan. *The Reconstruction of Georgia.* U of Minnesota P, 1966.

Currie-McDaniel, Ruth. *Carpetbagger of Conscience: A Biography of John Emory Bryant.* Fordham UP, 1999.

Downs, Gregory P. *After Appomattox*. Harvard UP, 2015.

Edwards, Rem B, Jr. *Bios Edwards, Thomas J. and Mary Jane Portwood Jarrett Edwards*. USGenWeb Archives, 2008.

Hightower, Edward O. *Convicted and Railroaded: Rufus B. Bullock and Georgia Convict Leasing, 1868-1871*. Clark Atlanta UP, 2011.

Library of Congress. *Alexander Hamilton Stephens Papers, 1784-1886*.

---. *Slave Narratives: A Folk History of Slavery in the United States from Interviews with Former Slave*s. Federal Writers' Project, 1936-1938.

Schott, Thomas E. *Alexander H. Stephens of Georgia: A Biography*. Louisiana State UP, 1988.

Thompson, C. Mildred. *Reconstruction in Georgia: Economic, Social, Political 1865-1872*. Columbia UP, 1915.

United States Congressional Serial Set. Vol. 1237. Government Printing Office, 1866.

Willingham, Robert M, Jr. *The History of Wilkes County, Georgia*. Wilkes, 2002.

Made in the USA
Columbia, SC
14 November 2017